10 STEP
WATERCOLOUR

—

BIRDS

Published in 2022 by Search Press Ltd.
Wellwood, North Farm Road
Tunbridge Wells
Kent TN2 3DR

This book is produced by
The Bright Press,
an imprint of the Quarto Group,
The Old Brewery, 6 Blundell Street,
London N7 9BH, United Kingdom.
T (0)20 7700 6700
www.QuartoKnows.com

ISBN: 978-1-80092-008-8
ebook ISBN: 978-1-80093-001-8

Publisher: James Evans
Editorial Director: Isheeta Mustafi
Art Director: James Lawrence
Managing Editor: Jacqui Sayers
Editor: Emily Angus
Project Editor: Anna Southgate
Designer: Emma Clayton

Printed and bound in China

MIX
Paper from
responsible sources
FSC® C016973
FSC
www.fsc.org

10 STEP
WATERCOLOUR

BIRDS

PAINT 25 EXQUISITELY DETAILED
BIRDS IN 10 EASY STEPS

ELEANOR LONGHURST

Search Press

CONTENTS

1 GETTING STARTED

INTRODUCTION

I have always been fascinated by birds. Their beautiful, intricate patterns
and delicate feathers lend themselves naturally to watercolours.

I grew up watching the goldfinches and sparrows in my garden, and always
had a paint set nearby to capture them. Much of this book was painted to
the sound of blackbirds chirping outside the window of my sunny plant-
filled flat. My cat took great interest in all the reference images of birds on
my computer screen!

I am a self-taught watercolour painter, having started as a small child. My
style of painting is not quite the traditional watercolour method – I use far
more pigment and less water than the norm, creating tight illustrations,
focusing on small details rather than using large, sweeping washes of colour.
So, the projects in this book might seem rather different at first.

Bird illustrations have formed an integral part of my business, Little Paisley
Designs, since starting in 2014. My bird paintings have been turned into
many different products, such as enamel pins and notebooks, and sent all
over the world. I have loved introducing British wildlife to a whole new
audience, mixing illustrations of British flora and fauna with colourful
modern patterns and products to appeal to a much wider audience.
I hope this book continues in the same vein.

My work focuses primarily on British nature, so it has been lovely
to explore species from further afield for this book, to offer you
a really colourful mix of birds from around the world,
with a variety of sizes and poses.

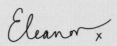

HOW TO USE THIS BOOK

Arranged in three chapters based on skill level, this book features twenty-five projects, each one showing you how to paint a bird in ten steps. You can pick and choose which birds to paint. If you are a beginner, however, it would be a good idea to start with one or two easy projects to build your confidence before moving on.

Useful tips offer advice on working methods and techniques.

Each project has a skill rating: easy, moderate or advanced.

Swatches show the colours you need to mix for each step.

Numbers beside the colour swatches
tell you which brush sizes to use.

BUILDING CONFIDENCE

GREAT TIT

Brush 1 & 000
Payne's Gray

7

DEEPER GREYS

Mix Payne's gray with a little water. Fill the beak, using a more concentrated colour on the top section. Paint each grey section of the wing, varying the tone. Switch to the 000 brush and add an outline and shadow lines on the legs and feet, using minimal water.

8

BOLDER COLOURS

Mix a concentrated burnt umber and ivory black for the eye. Add Payne's gray to the green base colour and paint short strokes over the lighter green. Mix yellow ochre with a little water to paint long strokes over the yellow belly, working in different directions to create a fluffy look. Mix lots of water with Payne's gray and apply to the pale face and tail patches using short strokes.

After adding each new layer of colour, wash water over the lines using a size 1 brush to blend in the colour.

Brush 000
Burnt Umber and
Ivory Black

Brush 000
Olive Green,
Sap Green,
Payne's Gray

Brush 000
Yellow Ochre

Brush 000
Payne's Gray

92

Brush 000, 1 & 5/0
Ivory Black and Payne's Gray

9

DARK OUTLINES

Mix ivory black and Payne's gray with a little water, then brush long strokes down and around the tail. Add small strokes that follow the curves of the black head and belly areas to create texture. Use the size 1 brush to wash water over the strokes to blend them in. With water on your brush, trace around the lines on the wing. Mix a concentrated ivory black and use the size 5/0 brush to outline the brown eye. Draw a darker black circle within the brown eye.

10

PALE HIGHLIGHTS

Use a size 5/0 brush to add white drawing ink highlights in and around the eye and on the light face and tail patches. Add lines to divide the beak and give it an outline. Add a few highlights to the breast and underbelly and paint over the white details on the wing and tail. Finally, sketch in a pencil branch for your bird to perch on.

93

The finished painting serves as a
reference to guide you as you work.

USING WATERCOLOURS

All projects in this book use the same materials and work in the same way. Many of the steps use the same techniques no matter which bird you are painting. Read through this section closely before starting a project and refer back to these pages if you need any reminders on which tools and techniques to use while working.

CHOOSING MATERIALS

Each bird is painted on a sheet of A5 paper, using the same twenty-four-pan paint set and palette, and a range of brushes in five sizes.

PAPER

I use cold-pressed watercolour paper, as I have a particular affection for its hammered texture and ability to soak up the paint. If you prefer the grain of the paper not to show through in your paintings, opt for hot-pressed watercolour paper, which is smooth.

The size of paper I use measures around 15 x 21cm (5¾in x 8⅓in), and I prefer a good, heavyweight thickness (300gsm). It means you can paint on both sides without colour bleeding through, which is excellent for practising. My style of painting involves using more pigment and less water than traditional watercolour painting, and so the paper is less likely to warp.

PENCIL

I use a regular HB pencil to carry out all of the drawing stages in these projects, and a good-quality pencil sharpener to keep the tip pointed.

PAINTS

Watercolour paints come in sets containing small blocks of concentrated pigment called pans. I use a Winsor & Newton Professional Watercolour set with twenty-four half pans. The quality is far superior to anything else I have tried, and the pigments so rich. But they are rather pricey. If you are a beginner, a Winsor & Newton Cotman Watercolour set is a great entry-level option. The colour names I use in this book (see below) are found in the professional set, but I have included swatches of my mixes beside each step so you can create colours that best match them. As you become more skilled at painting with

| Lemon Yellow | Winsor Yellow | Aureolin | Winsor Orange | Winsor Red | Permanent Alizarin Crimson | Permanent Rose | Cerulean Blue |

| Winsor Violet | Winsor Blue | French Ultramarine | Prussian Blue | Indigo | Olive Green | Permanent Sap Green | Viridian |

| Yellow Ochre | Raw Sienna | Burnt Sienna | Raw Umber | Burnt Umber | Payne's Gray | Ivory Black | Chinese White |

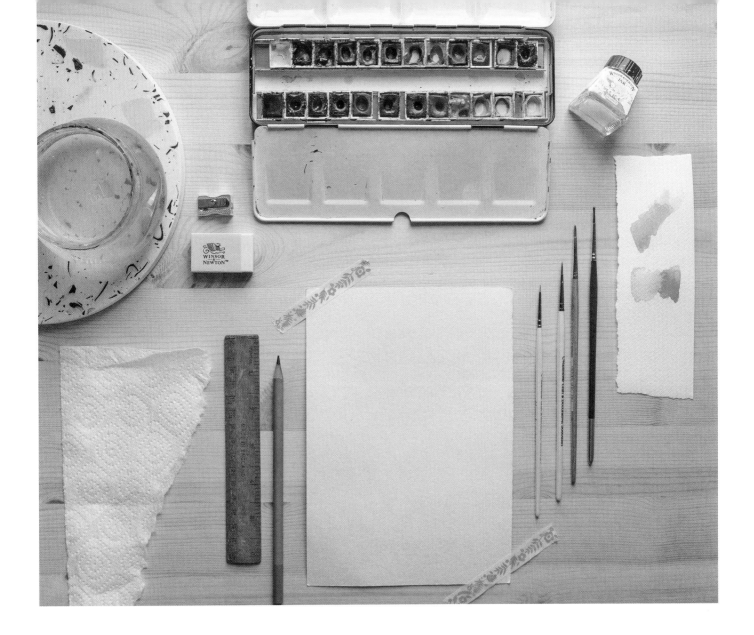

watercolours, it is worth investing in quality paints – you will use less pigment and they can last you a lifetime.

I like to finish my paintings with a layer of fine detail using white Winsor & Newton Drawing Ink. This is particularly good for creating highlights on the birds that have more complex markings, such as the hummingbird, the kingfisher and the pigeon. As an alternative to the white drawing ink, you can mix Chinese white watercolour pigment with a little water to achieve the same results.

It is important to take care of your paint palette, to keep it looking its best. When you need to change colours, always clean your brush between dipping. If you accidentally mix colours within the pans and your yellow has green paint in it – this is easily done – just add a little water to the pan, and dab with a piece of paper towel until the paint pan is back to its original colour.

PAINTBRUSHES

I have used five brush sizes for the projects in this book, and prefer pointed round brushes because they are very flexible and allow for a wide range of brushstrokes. The brushes are Pro Arte Masterstroke brushes in sizes 2 and 0, and Cass Art synthetic round brushes in sizes 1, 000 and 5/0. All of the effects featured in the projects can be achieved using these brushes.

Whichever brushes you choose to use, make sure you take care of them. Keep them clean and they will last. Once you have finished using a brush, do not leave it standing in water. This will make the paint on the handle splinter over time, and you will split the bristles. Instead, once you have finished with a colour, simply dip the brush in water, swill it around, dab with a paper towel and leave to dry on a new sheet of paper towel.

OTHER EQUIPMENT

There are several other pieces of equipment that you will find very useful. The first is an artist-quality eraser. This is important for removing pencil lines from your sketches without damaging the paper. When erasing pencil lines, always move your eraser in the same direction as the pencil lines and press lightly and slowly, keeping one hand firmly on the paper to hold it in place.

I always keep a large stack of paper towels on my desk, which I use for a wide range of purposes, including wiping colour off my brush, drying my brushes and dabbing my painting as I work. In this last role, the paper is not only invaluable when it comes to removing mistakes, but can be used to great effect in creating a range of textured effects by dabbing away at a wet paint layer.

Another key piece of kit is a vessel for holding your water. I use an old glass jar. Make sure your vessel has a wide base so you cannot knock it over and is not so tall that you can lose your brush in it. Crucially, use a vessel made from clear glass or plastic so that you can see when you need to change the water. Do this frequently throughout a painting session, to keep your colour mixes bright and as you intend them.

WORKSPACE

Always try to paint in natural daylight. Your colours will look better, and you will be able to see what you are doing more clearly. If you cannot dedicate space to painting alone, clear some room on a desk or dining table and have everything you need within reach.

DRAWING TECHNIQUES

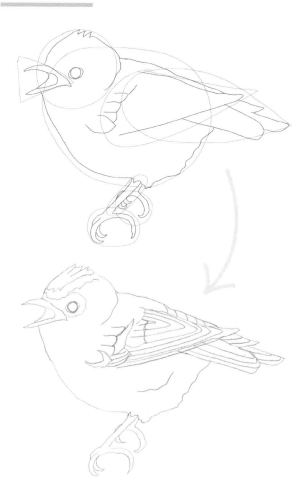

I start each project by drawing shapes that capture the basic form and position of the bird. In most projects this is a series of teardrop and circle shapes that represent the different body parts and their relative proportions. With these in place, I refine the outline and draw in all the details I want to paint – feather layers, facial features and changes of colour.

I prefer my finished paintings to have only the faintest trace of pencil in them. Once I have an outline I like, I go over the lines again, pressing hard. Erasing the pencil slowly and carefully leaves me with a faint line and an indent that acts as an invisible border for the paint.

MIXING WATERCOLOURS

• Always use a clean palette to mix your colours.

• Your brush should always be wet. Even the most concentrated colour needs a wet brush in order to create fluid lines. Too little water will cause the pigment to run out, resulting in broken lines.

• Start with the lightest of two (or more) colours you plan to mix together. Add lots of water to your brush, dab this on an empty section of the paint palette, then sweep the brush over the first pan of dry colour. Add enough pigment to the water on the palette to make quite a concentrated colour. Clean your brush and sweep over the next pan of dry colour. Little by little add this, and other colours, to the first, until you have achieved the shade you want.

• Mix more paint than you think you will need, using a larger paintbrush than you plan to use. It can be difficult to replicate the exact shade if you need to mix more.

• Remember, you can always add more water to thin the paint mix, or more pigment to make the colour more concentrated.

• Keep a piece of scrap watercolour paper on your desk to test how different colours look before you apply them to your painting. I tend to use the smoother, hot-pressed watercolour paper for this.

• Once you are painting, if you add too much water, you can always dab at the paint lightly with a paper towel. This is much easier than having to stop your flow to add more water to the brush.

| Tiny amount of water | A little water | More water | Lots of water | Tiny amount of paint | Paint after dabbing with a paper towel (right) |

VARYING AMOUNTS OF WATER

You will see that I use quite concentrated colours. In fact, when I instruct you to use a 'concentrated' mix of any colour, this still has water blended in – just in tiny amounts. As you add more water, the colours you make become less and less opaque.

FIXING MISTAKES

If you make a mistake while painting, dab the paint as quickly as possible with a paper towel to remove it. If the paint has already dried, dip a clean brush in water and dab away at the paint to remove it.

BASIC WORKING METHODS

WORKING WET-ON-DRY

For the majority of projects in this book, the steps are painted using the wet-on-dry method. This means letting the paint dry before adding another layer of wet paint on top of, or next to, a painted section. This allows you to build layers of colour gradually, and to paint different colours beside each other without them bleeding into one another. It is important to let the paint dry between colours to keep the painting looking neat and to allow clear definition. Do not try to rush the process by using a hairdryer or popping the paper on a radiator, as this will cause the paint to run and the paper to warp.

Wet next to wet (blended)

Wet next to dry (no bleed)

WORKING WET-ON-WET

For some of the projects, you will apply wet paint on top of, or next to, a wet paint section so that the colours blend together. This is called the wet-on-wet method. It does not allow as much control, but can create some lovely soft textures. I usually work wet-on-wet in the first few steps of a painting, to create a blended base on which to add detail.

WORKING DRY-ON-DRY

Using a very concentrated paint on top of a dry layer introduces a more textured finish.

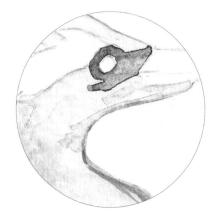

Wet-on-wet

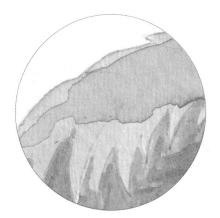

Wet-on-dry

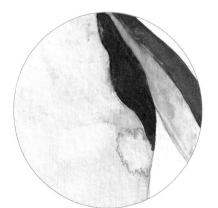

Wet-on-wet, with dabbing

Dry-on-dry

BRUSHSTROKES

I usually use the largest of my brushes (2 and 1) to apply the first washes of colour, and the smallest brushes (000 or 5/0) for the finer details. You will find the appropriate brush sizes alongside the colour swatches that I give with each step.

You can achieve a wide variety of thicknesses with each of the brushes, by varying the amount of pressure you place on them. Using scrap paper and paint with plenty of water, take some time to get to know the different strokes you can achieve. Tilting the brush at different angles allows you to create a range of effects. A thick brushstroke with a thin tapered end is easily achievable using a long, pointed brush, such as a size 2. Simply apply less pressure to the brushstroke as the line progresses.

Some projects require a series of 'V' shapes on the feathers. Paint these quickly, with a thin, pointed line flowing down to a thicker curve, and back up to a thin point.

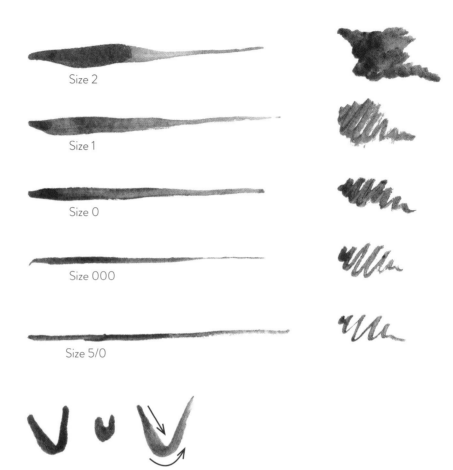

Size 2

Size 1

Size 0

Size 000

Size 5/0

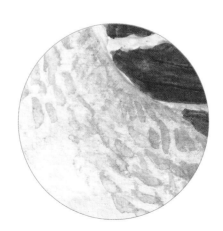

Larger brushes are best suited to washes and broader brushstrokes.

Small brushes can be fiddly at first, but are easy to correct if you make a mistake, as the marks are smaller.

USEFUL TECHNIQUES

I have used a wide range of techniques, not only to capture the natural shapes and colours of the birds, but also to mimic their different types of feathers and markings. Experiment with these methods and use them in different ways to create light and dark tones, to capture texture and to master three-dimensionality.

FIRST WASH

Most birds have a base body colour. I apply this using a size 2 brush and plenty of water. By varying the amount of pigment and/or water you use, you can create a range of different tones. Your work does not have to be neat at this stage.

LAYERING

Many steps involve building layers to create depth in a painting. I often layer washes of different colours on top of one another to create one rich colour. For example, I might layer yellow and brown to create a deeper brown.

SHORT FEATHERS

To create short feathers, I use fine brushstrokes, all running in the same direction. On a bird's neck, I keep the lines shorter and closer together at the top of the neck, but make them longer and further apart towards the bottom.

BUILDING TEXTURE

Some birds, such as the northern cardinal and the long-tailed tit, have slightly longer, almost fluffy feathers. For these, I add the paint by brushing loosely in different directions, crisscrossing the lines to create texture.

SHAPE AND TONE

To give legs and feet a three-dimensional appearance, I leave a base layer of colour to dry before adding a second, darker colour. I use the darker colour to outline the legs and to paint thin, horizontal curves to create tone.

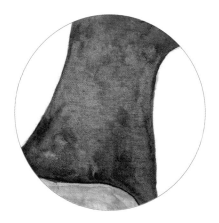

IRIDESCENCE

I use the wet-on-wet method to create the iridescence of birds such as the pigeon and the hummingbird. This involves working quickly to add one colour after the next while the previous layers are still wet. You can then encourage the colours to run into each other so they blend.

FINE MARKINGS

Some of the birds, such as the blue jay and the American kestrel, have very detailed tail and wing feathers. These are painted after several washes and a few layers of colour, and using the smallest brush sizes. I always keep the finest details to the top two layers of a painting.

WHITE OUTLINES AND HIGHLIGHTS

I like to add outlines and highlights using a small, pointed paintbrush and either white Winsor & Newton Drawing Ink or a concentrated mix of Chinese white watercolour paint. This is optional, but I find it really makes the colours pop.

DISPLAYING YOUR WORK

Pop some washi tape on the corner of a finished painting for a quick way to display it on a wall. Several paintings from a collection of similar projects look great displayed this way. If you plan to mount and/or frame your finished paintings, bear in mind that you might want to use a larger paper size to allow for an even border all the way around the bird within the frame.

1

GETTING STARTED

Here is a collection of easy, approachable projects to get you started. All of the birds in this chapter have fairly simplistic poses and plumage in one or two colours, and large markings. You can do most of the painting using the bigger paintbrush sizes to apply sweeping washes of colour, and there is little need for intricate line details.

ATLANTIC PUFFIN
Fratercula arctica

The puffin has simple black-and-white markings, so is a great project to start with.
The beak and feet add beautiful splashes of colour against the monochrome.

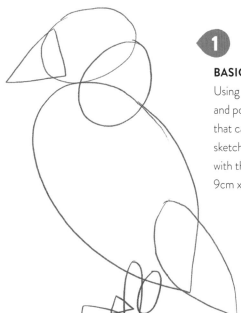

1

BASIC FORM

Using light pencil strokes, and following the proportions and positions in my sketch, draw a series of shapes that capture the puffin's basic form. For reference, my sketch is roughly 16cm tall by 12cm wide (6¼in x 4¾in), with the teardrop-shaped body measuring around 9cm x 7cm (3½in x 2¾in).

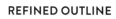

2

REFINED OUTLINE

Sketch a more accurate outline within your basic shapes. Notice how curved the puffin's beak is, and how its top is much larger than its bottom. A puffin's breast is puffed out slightly, so the upper section of the body is much wider than the lower section. The wings are slim and pointed. The feet are large and webbed. Once happy with your outline, erase the basic shapes.

3

PENCIL DETAILS

Using the final image as a reference, draw in more detail to distinguish the bird's markings. Outline the different coloured sections of the beak and add a few lines on the wings to draw out changes of colour. Go over the lines once more, pressing hard to create an indent to use as a border for the paint.

4

PENCIL IMPRESSION

Erase the pencil lines, leaving just the indent and very light pencil strokes. Alternatively, if you prefer to leave a few pencil marks on the page, make sure you will be happy with them showing through the paint.

5

DARKEST TONES

Add Payne's gray to ivory black with just enough water for a concentrated but opaque mix. Use this to paint the first section of the beak. Add more water and cover the top of the head, below the face and the bird's back, wings and tail. Allow the paint to bleed into the water a little to create texture.

Brush 2
Payne's Gray
and Ivory Black

Paint one section at a time and vary the amount of water on your brush to make some sections darker than others. Allow each layer to dry before painting the next.

6

LIGHTEST TONES

Mix Chinese white with plenty of water and a tiny amount of Payne's gray. Use this to paint the section of the head around the eye, the bird's belly and the underside of the tail and wing. While the paint is still wet, add a little more Payne's gray to the mix and paint over the wet white paint where it meets the edges of the black on the wing and underbelly.

Brush 2
Chinese White
and Payne's Gray

Brush 1
Burnt Sienna

Brush 1
Raw Umber

7

COLOUR FOUNDATIONS

Mix a concentrated burnt sienna for painting the legs and feet. Add more water, and paint just the three raised toes to distinguish them from the webbed sections. Apply a watery layer at the very tip of the beak. Mix raw umber with lots of water and make short, dotted strokes over the pale grey section near the wing and under the tail. Apply the same technique on the bird's face to create a mottled effect. This is a good way to show texture without complicated brushstrokes.

8

LEGS, BEAK AND FACE

Mix burnt sienna and Winsor red with lots of water and dab short strokes up the backs of both legs. Add more water to the brush to blend the strokes in. Use the same colour to fill the webbed sections of the feet. Add the following stripes on the beak, leaving the base layer showing through in places: a watery Winsor red for the tip; a burnt sienna/Winsor red mix; a watery Winsor orange; and a bright, opaque aureolin where the beak meets the head. Use the burnt sienna/Winsor red mix to paint a thin line down the middle of the beak. Use a concentrated mix of Winsor red to outline the eye. Mix Payne's gray and ivory black with plenty of water to add the distinctive patch around the eye.

Brush 0
Burnt Sienna
and Winsor Red

Brush 0
Aureolin

Brush 0
Winsor Red

Brush 0
Winsor Orange

Brush 0
Payne's Gray
and Ivory Black

Brush 000
Ivory Black

9

FEATHER DETAILS

Mix a concentrated ivory black. Fill in the eye and paint the claws using one long, curved brushstroke for each. Give the wings and tail an outline and paint a series of curved lines to suggest sections of feathers.

10

SETTING THE SCENE

Add in the suggestion of a background. Using a pencil, lightly sketch out a series of rock shapes. Add texture to the rocks with scribbly lines, crosshatching and shading. Add sprigs of grass to complete the picture.

There's something wonderful about a bright, colourful watercolour painting set on a sketched pencil background that adds just the slightest suggestion of the landscape the bird inhabits.

TOCO TOUCAN

Ramphastos toco

One of the world's most recognizable birds, the toucan's large,
brightly coloured beak and tuxedo jacket plumage make it stand out.

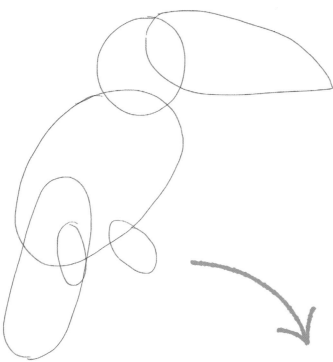

1

BASIC FORM

Using light pencil strokes, and following
the proportions and positions in my sketch,
draw a series of shapes that capture the
toucan's form. For reference, my sketch
is 13cm tall by 13cm wide (5in x 5in), with
the oval for the body measuring around
9cm x 6cm (3½in x 2¾in).

2

REFINED OUTLINE

Sketch a more accurate outline within
your basic shapes. Notice how the bird's
head and neck are long, with a clear
distinction between them and the body.
The tail is short and flat along the bottom;
the wings are flush with the body. The
bird has short legs and long, thin feet.
Once happy with your outline, erase
the basic shapes.

*If adding a twig, as in Step 10, it could help to sketch
it in at this stage, to take account of perspective.*

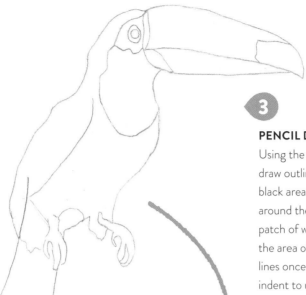

3

PENCIL DETAILS

Using the final image as a reference, draw outlines for sections of colour: the black areas on the beak; the orange patch around the eye and the blue iris; the large patch of white on the bird's throat; and the area of red under the tail. Go over the lines once more, pressing hard to create an indent to use as a border for the paint.

4

PENCIL IMPRESSION

Erase the pencil lines, leaving just the indent and very light pencil strokes. Alternatively, if you prefer to leave a few pencil marks on the page, make sure you will be happy with them showing through the paint.

Brush 2
Payne's Gray
and Ivory Black

5

BODY COLOUR

Mix Payne's gray and ivory black with a little water to create a semi-transparent paint. Apply this using long, flowing sweeps to paint the top of the bird's head, its body and tail. Paint the wing area once the belly has dried slightly so the two don't bleed together; a natural line will form between the two areas.

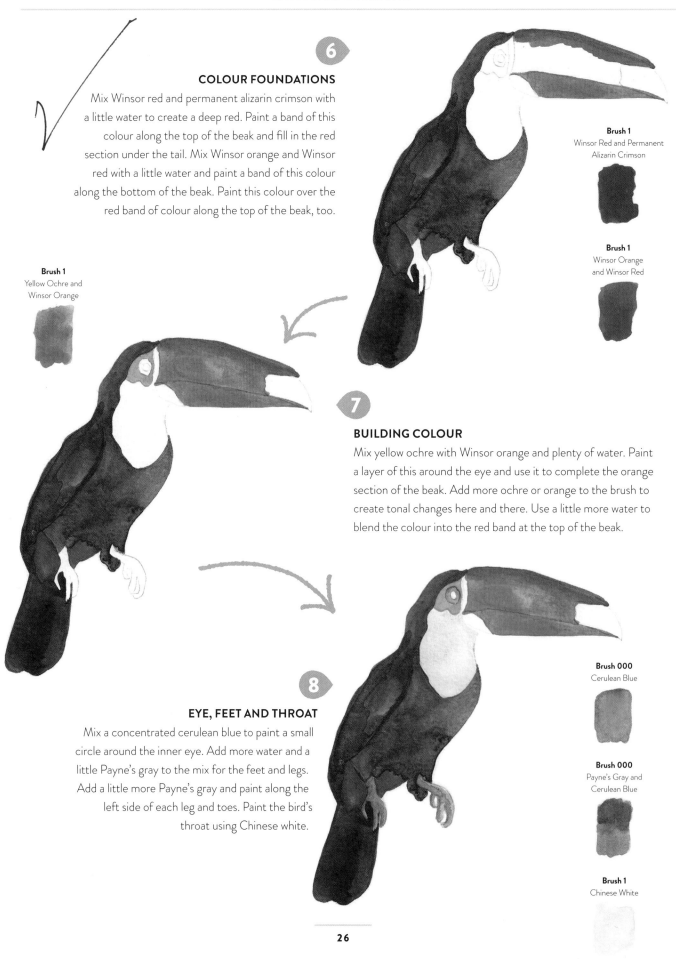

6

COLOUR FOUNDATIONS

Mix Winsor red and permanent alizarin crimson with a little water to create a deep red. Paint a band of this colour along the top of the beak and fill in the red section under the tail. Mix Winsor orange and Winsor red with a little water and paint a band of this colour along the bottom of the beak. Paint this colour over the red band of colour along the top of the beak, too.

Brush 1
Winsor Red and Permanent Alizarin Crimson

Brush 1
Winsor Orange and Winsor Red

Brush 1
Yellow Ochre and Winsor Orange

7

BUILDING COLOUR

Mix yellow ochre with Winsor orange and plenty of water. Paint a layer of this around the eye and use it to complete the orange section of the beak. Add more ochre or orange to the brush to create tonal changes here and there. Use a little more water to blend the colour into the red band at the top of the beak.

8

EYE, FEET AND THROAT

Mix a concentrated cerulean blue to paint a small circle around the inner eye. Add more water and a little Payne's gray to the mix for the feet and legs. Add a little more Payne's gray and paint along the left side of each leg and toes. Paint the bird's throat using Chinese white.

Brush 000
Cerulean Blue

Brush 000
Payne's Gray and Cerulean Blue

Brush 1
Chinese White

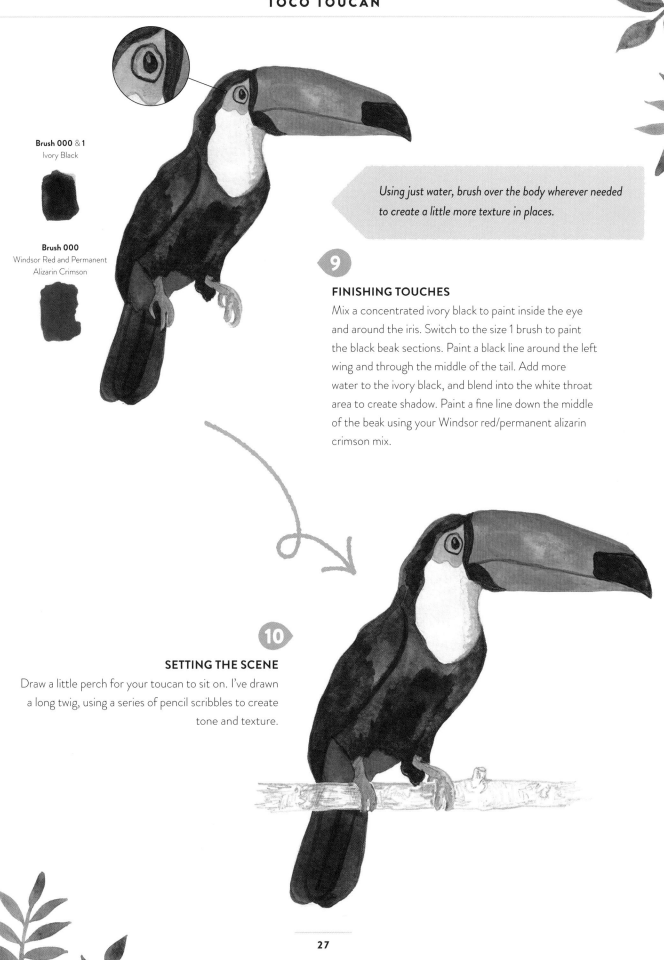

Brush 000 & 1
Ivory Black

Brush 000
Windsor Red and Permanent
Alizarin Crimson

Using just water, brush over the body wherever needed to create a little more texture in places.

9

FINISHING TOUCHES

Mix a concentrated ivory black to paint inside the eye and around the iris. Switch to the size 1 brush to paint the black beak sections. Paint a black line around the left wing and through the middle of the tail. Add more water to the ivory black, and blend into the white throat area to create shadow. Paint a fine line down the middle of the beak using your Windsor red/permanent alizarin crimson mix.

10

SETTING THE SCENE

Draw a little perch for your toucan to sit on. I've drawn a long twig, using a series of pencil scribbles to create tone and texture.

AMERICAN FLAMINGO

Phoenicopterus ruber

In this project you will use the wet-on-wet method to let the coral pink colours of the flamingo blend together, creating beautiful tones.

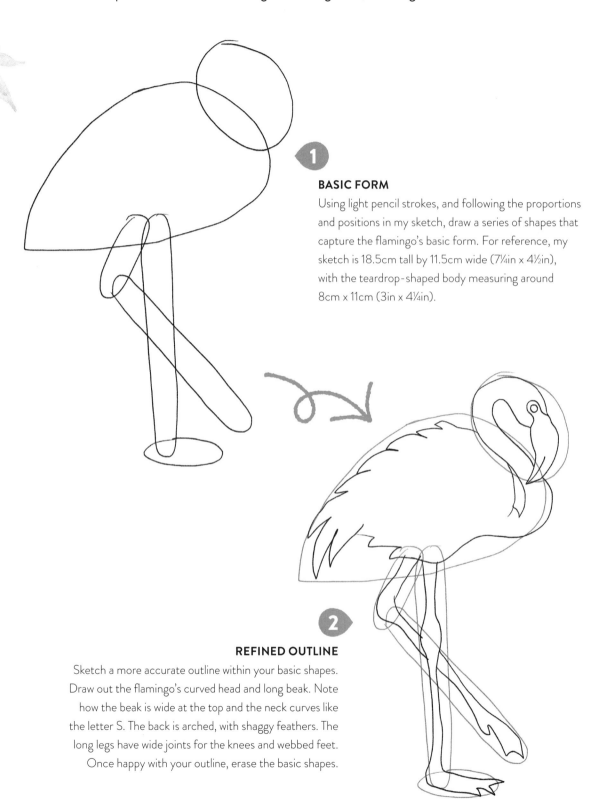

1

BASIC FORM

Using light pencil strokes, and following the proportions and positions in my sketch, draw a series of shapes that capture the flamingo's basic form. For reference, my sketch is 18.5cm tall by 11.5cm wide (7¼in x 4½in), with the teardrop-shaped body measuring around 8cm x 11cm (3in x 4¼in).

2

REFINED OUTLINE

Sketch a more accurate outline within your basic shapes. Draw out the flamingo's curved head and long beak. Note how the beak is wide at the top and the neck curves like the letter S. The back is arched, with shaggy feathers. The long legs have wide joints for the knees and webbed feet. Once happy with your outline, erase the basic shapes.

PENCIL DETAILS

Add more detail within the bird's outline. Draw lines to mark the black and white areas of the beak. Add more feather detail along the top of the bird's back, with longer feathers for the tail. Add a section of feathers to distinguish the wing, and neaten up the feet and legs. Go over the lines once more, pressing hard with your pencil to create an indent to use as a border for the paint.

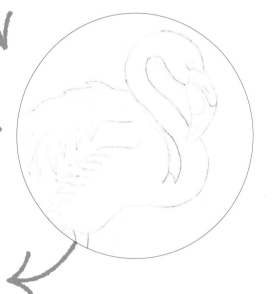

PENCIL IMPRESSION

Erase the pencil lines, leaving just the indent and very light pencil strokes. If you prefer to leave a few pencil marks on the page, make sure you will be happy with them showing through the paint.

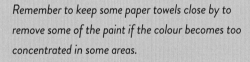

Remember to keep some paper towels close by to remove some of the paint if the colour becomes too concentrated in some areas.

BODY COLOUR

Mix aureolin and permanent rose with lots of water. Paint a watery layer over the head and body of your bird. Use more water for the top feathers and more pigment for the tail and underbelly. Let the pigment blend into the water on the page, creating different tones.

Brush 2
Aureolin and
Permanent Rose

29

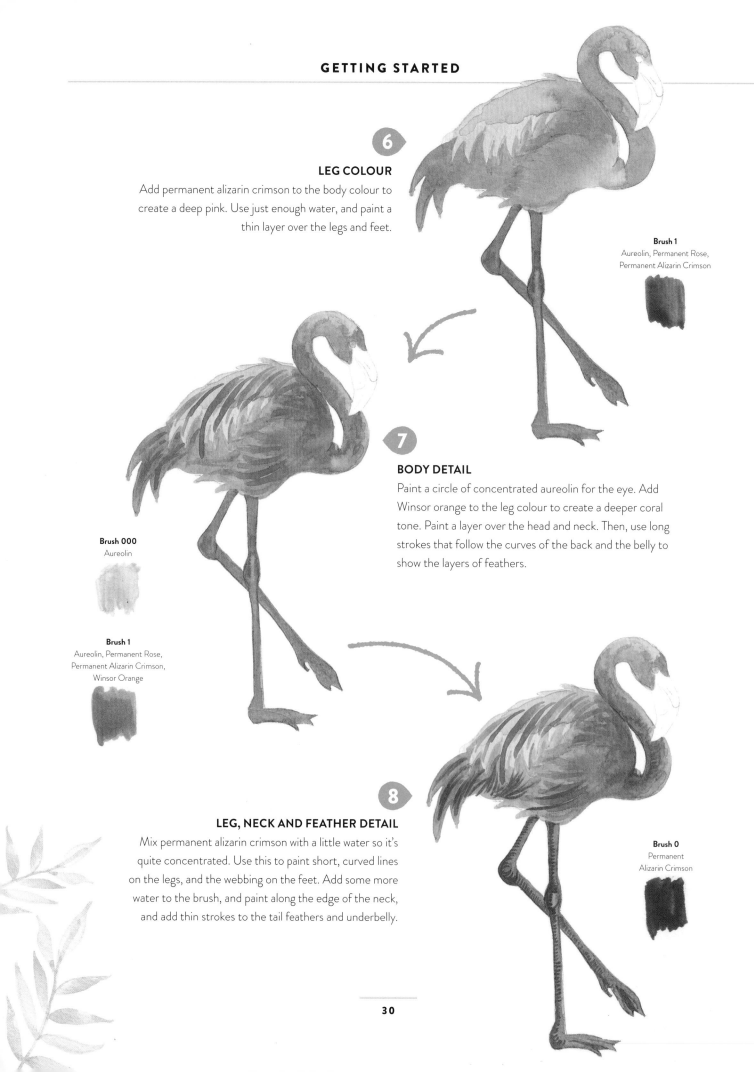

6

LEG COLOUR

Add permanent alizarin crimson to the body colour to create a deep pink. Use just enough water, and paint a thin layer over the legs and feet.

Brush 1
Aureolin, Permanent Rose, Permanent Alizarin Crimson

7

BODY DETAIL

Paint a circle of concentrated aureolin for the eye. Add Winsor orange to the leg colour to create a deeper coral tone. Paint a layer over the head and neck. Then, use long strokes that follow the curves of the back and the belly to show the layers of feathers.

Brush 000
Aureolin

Brush 1
Aureolin, Permanent Rose, Permanent Alizarin Crimson, Winsor Orange

LEG, NECK AND FEATHER DETAIL

Mix permanent alizarin crimson with a little water so it's quite concentrated. Use this to paint short, curved lines on the legs, and the webbing on the feet. Add some more water to the brush, and paint along the edge of the neck, and add thin strokes to the tail feathers and underbelly.

8

Brush 0
Permanent Alizarin Crimson

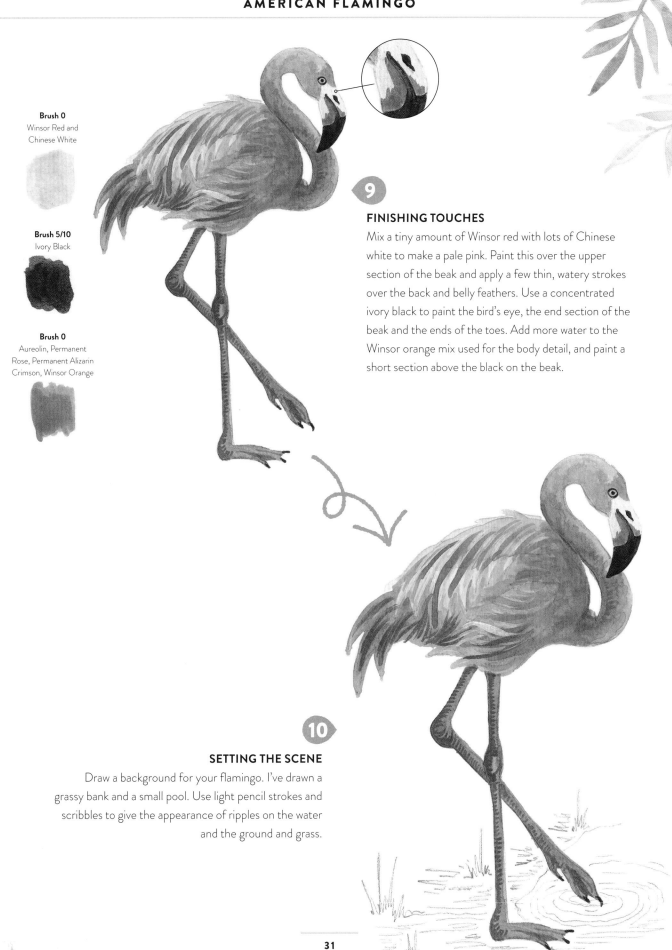

Brush 0
Winsor Red and
Chinese White

Brush 5/10
Ivory Black

Brush 0
Aureolin, Permanent
Rose, Permanent Alizarin
Crimson, Winsor Orange

9

FINISHING TOUCHES

Mix a tiny amount of Winsor red with lots of Chinese white to make a pale pink. Paint this over the upper section of the beak and apply a few thin, watery strokes over the back and belly feathers. Use a concentrated ivory black to paint the bird's eye, the end section of the beak and the ends of the toes. Add more water to the Winsor orange mix used for the body detail, and paint a short section above the black on the beak.

10

SETTING THE SCENE

Draw a background for your flamingo. I've drawn a grassy bank and a small pool. Use light pencil strokes and scribbles to give the appearance of ripples on the water and the ground and grass.

ROCKHOPPER PENGUIN

Eudyptes chrysocome

The smallest of the crested penguins, the rockhopper has a delicate feather crown on its head, and some very fetching yellow eyebrows.

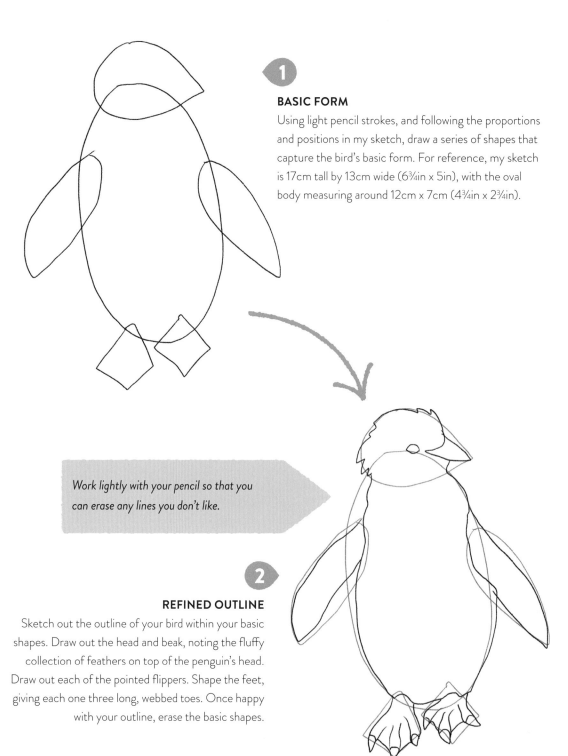

1
BASIC FORM

Using light pencil strokes, and following the proportions and positions in my sketch, draw a series of shapes that capture the bird's basic form. For reference, my sketch is 17cm tall by 13cm wide (6¾in x 5in), with the oval body measuring around 12cm x 7cm (4¾in x 2¾in).

Work lightly with your pencil so that you can erase any lines you don't like.

2
REFINED OUTLINE

Sketch out the outline of your bird within your basic shapes. Draw out the head and beak, noting the fluffy collection of feathers on top of the penguin's head. Draw out each of the pointed flippers. Shape the feet, giving each one three long, webbed toes. Once happy with your outline, erase the basic shapes.

PENCIL DETAILS

Using the final image as a reference, add more detail within the outline. Define the colourful mane of feathers on top of the head and where the chest and flippers change colour. Go over the lines once more, pressing hard with your pencil to create an indent to use as a border for the paint.

PENCIL IMPRESSION

Erase the pencil lines, leaving just the indent and very light pencil strokes. If you prefer to leave a few pencil marks on the page, make sure you will be happy with them showing through the paint.

Brush 2
Payne's Gray
and Ivory Black

DARKEST MARKINGS

Mix Payne's gray and ivory black with lots of water. Making sure the mix is very wet, paint long strokes over the top of the head, face, neck and the edges of the flippers. Allow the paint to flow up to the indents you created. Paint thin, upward strokes on the top of the head for the feathers.

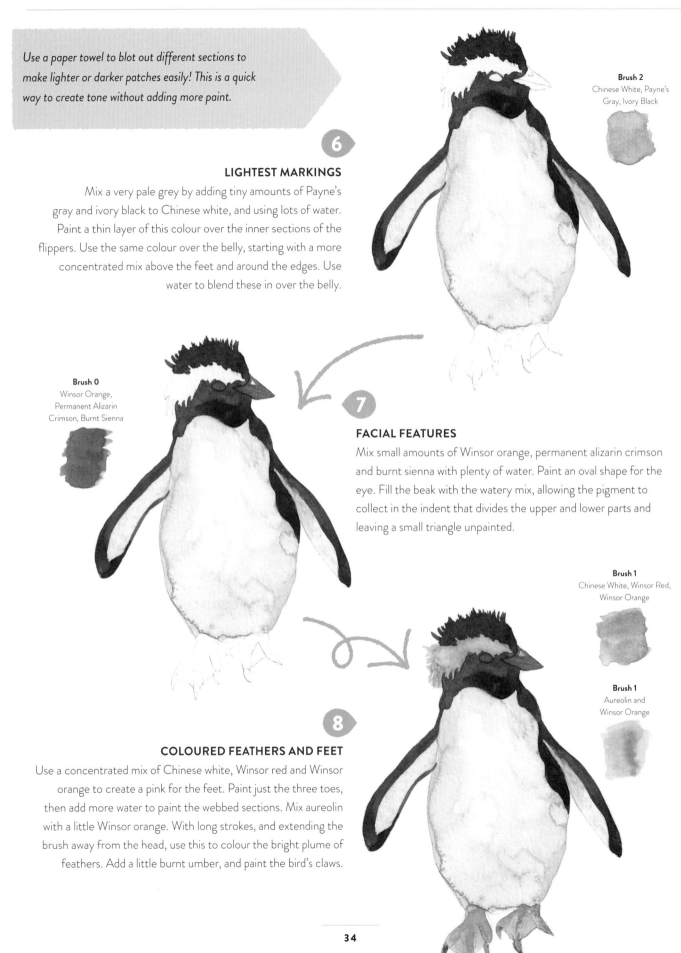

Use a paper towel to blot out different sections to make lighter or darker patches easily! This is a quick way to create tone without adding more paint.

Brush 2
Chinese White, Payne's Gray, Ivory Black

6 LIGHTEST MARKINGS

Mix a very pale grey by adding tiny amounts of Payne's gray and ivory black to Chinese white, and using lots of water. Paint a thin layer of this colour over the inner sections of the flippers. Use the same colour over the belly, starting with a more concentrated mix above the feet and around the edges. Use water to blend these in over the belly.

Brush 0
Winsor Orange, Permanent Alizarin Crimson, Burnt Sienna

7 FACIAL FEATURES

Mix small amounts of Winsor orange, permanent alizarin crimson and burnt sienna with plenty of water. Paint an oval shape for the eye. Fill the beak with the watery mix, allowing the pigment to collect in the indent that divides the upper and lower parts and leaving a small triangle unpainted.

Brush 1
Chinese White, Winsor Red, Winsor Orange

Brush 1
Aureolin and Winsor Orange

8 COLOURED FEATHERS AND FEET

Use a concentrated mix of Chinese white, Winsor red and Winsor orange to create a pink for the feet. Paint just the three toes, then add more water to paint the webbed sections. Mix aureolin with a little Winsor orange. With long strokes, and extending the brush away from the head, use this to colour the bright plume of feathers. Add a little burnt umber, and paint the bird's claws.

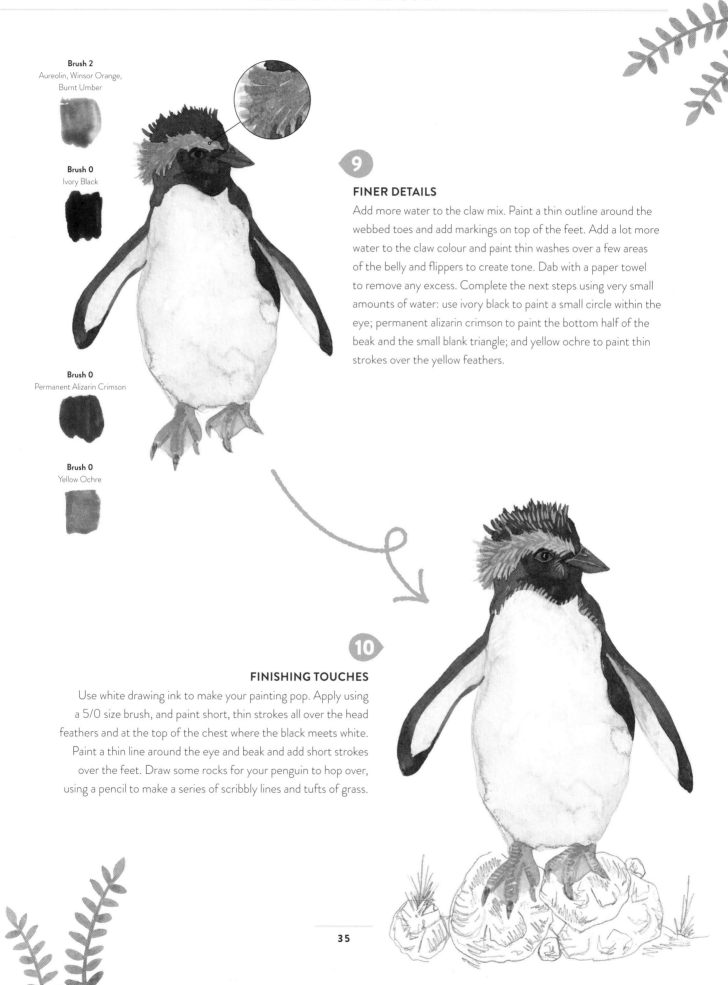

Brush 2
Aureolin, Winsor Orange, Burnt Umber

Brush 0
Ivory Black

Brush 0
Permanent Alizarin Crimson

Brush 0
Yellow Ochre

9 FINER DETAILS

Add more water to the claw mix. Paint a thin outline around the webbed toes and add markings on top of the feet. Add a lot more water to the claw colour and paint thin washes over a few areas of the belly and flippers to create tone. Dab with a paper towel to remove any excess. Complete the next steps using very small amounts of water: use ivory black to paint a small circle within the eye; permanent alizarin crimson to paint the bottom half of the beak and the small blank triangle; and yellow ochre to paint thin strokes over the yellow feathers.

10 FINISHING TOUCHES

Use white drawing ink to make your painting pop. Apply using a 5/0 size brush, and paint short, thin strokes all over the head feathers and at the top of the chest where the black meets white. Paint a thin line around the eye and beak and add short strokes over the feet. Draw some rocks for your penguin to hop over, using a pencil to make a series of scribbly lines and tufts of grass.

MUTE SWAN

Cygnus olor

Painting white onto a white background is difficult, so here you will use a mix of grey, brown and pink to give tone to the white paint.

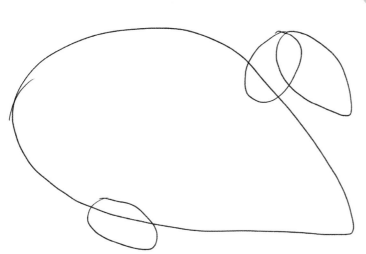

1

BASIC FORM

Using light pencil strokes, and following the proportions and positions in my sketch, draw a series of shapes that capture the swan's basic form. For reference, my sketch measures 18cm wide by 11cm tall (7in x 4¼in).

Note how the large oval body shape pretty much fills the dimensions of the whole sketch.

2

REFINED OUTLINE

Sketch a more accurate outline within your basic shapes. The head is small with a raised bump; the beak is long and flat. The neck has an S-shaped curve. The body is feathered, is flanked by two large, raised wings and ends in a pointed tail. Note how a small, webbed foot pokes out from beneath the body. Once you are happy with the outline, erase the basic shapes.

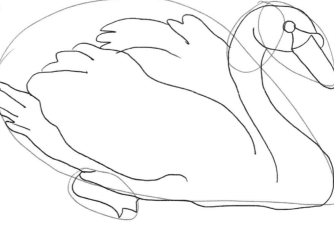

PENCIL DETAILS

Mark out the beak details and draw in more lines along the wings to show the separate feathers. Go over the lines once more, pressing hard with your pencil to create an indent to use as a border for the paint.

PENCIL IMPRESSION

Erase the pencil lines, leaving just the indent and very light pencil strokes. Alternatively, if you prefer to leave a few pencil marks on the page, make sure you will be happy with them showing through the paint.

BODY COLOUR

Mix Payne's gray with lots of water and use this to paint a watery base layer over the top of the head, body and wings. Leave the beak and webbed foot blank.

Brush 2
Payne's Gray

Dab this layer with a paper towel
if the colour is too concentrated.

 6

FEATHER LAYERS

Mix Payne's gray with burnt umber and lots
of water. Paint short, flat strokes over the
head and continue down the curve of the
neck, painting longer strokes as you go. Trace
the indented lines to paint long strokes that
follow the curves of each wing. Paint a series
of semi-circular strokes over the front wing to
show the feather layers.

Brush 2
Payne's Gray and
Burnt Umber

 7

TONE AND TEXTURE

Using lots of water, mix some permanent rose
into the feather mix and paint short strokes
over the body and wings. Add some Winsor
red to the mix, and brush short lines over the
wings to add texture. Mix ivory black with a
small amount of water for the facial features.

Brush 2
Payne's Gray, Burnt
Umber, Permanent Rose

Brush 2
Payne's Gray, Burnt Umber,
Permanent Rose, Winsor Red

Brush 0
Ivory Black

 8

BEAK AND FOOT

Mix permanent alizarin crimson and Winsor
orange with a little water. Paint this over the
beak. Paint the foot with a mix of ivory black
and a little permanent rose.

Brush 0
Permanent Alizarin Crimson
and Winsor Orange

Brush 0
Ivory Black and
Permanent Rose

Brush 000
Ivory Black

9

FINISHING TOUCHES

Mix ivory black with plenty of water, and add some highlight details over the neck and wings. Using white drawing ink and the same size brush, paint short strokes over the body, head, neck and wings. Add a thin white line over the top of the foot to show the webbed toes, and some detail over the heel. Paint a thin white line down the middle of the beak.

10

SETTING THE SCENE

Draw in some background for the bird. I've drawn some reeds and grassy sprigs on the riverbank, and added some ripples under the chest to indicate the water the bird is entering. Be loose and scruffy with your lines.

MALLARD

Anas platyrhynchos

This is a male mallard, known as a drake. Its markings are a beautiful colourful mix compared to the female of the species, which has brown speckled plumage.

1

BASIC FORM

Using light pencil strokes, and following the proportions and positions in my sketch, draw a series of shapes that capture the mid-flight form of the mallard. For reference, my sketch is 16cm tall by 14cm wide (6¼in x 5½in), with wing and body shapes of almost equal dimensions.

2

REFINED OUTLINE

Sketch a more accurate outline within your basic shapes. The body is thin and pointed, with small, curved feathers at the tail, and webbed feet close to the body. The head is flat and elongated, with a long, wide beak. The wings are wide with outstretched feathers – use long lines to show the different sections. Once happy with your outline, erase the basic shapes.

3 PENCIL DETAILS

Using the final image as a reference, draw outlines for different sections of colour: the dark-green head, the brown breast and the pale-brown body with areas of black and white. Mark the blue and black sections on the bird's far wing. Go over the lines once more, pressing hard to create an indent to use as a border for the paint.

4 PENCIL IMPRESSION

Erase the pencil lines, leaving just the indent and very light pencil strokes. Alternatively, if you prefer to leave a few pencil marks on the page, make sure you will be happy with them showing through the paint.

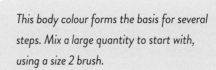

This body colour forms the basis for several steps. Mix a large quantity to start with, using a size 2 brush.

Brush 1
Ivory Black and
Burnt Umber

5 BODY COLOUR

Mix ivory black with burnt umber and lots of water. Wash a thin layer of colour over the belly, back, upper far wing and the underside of the near wing.

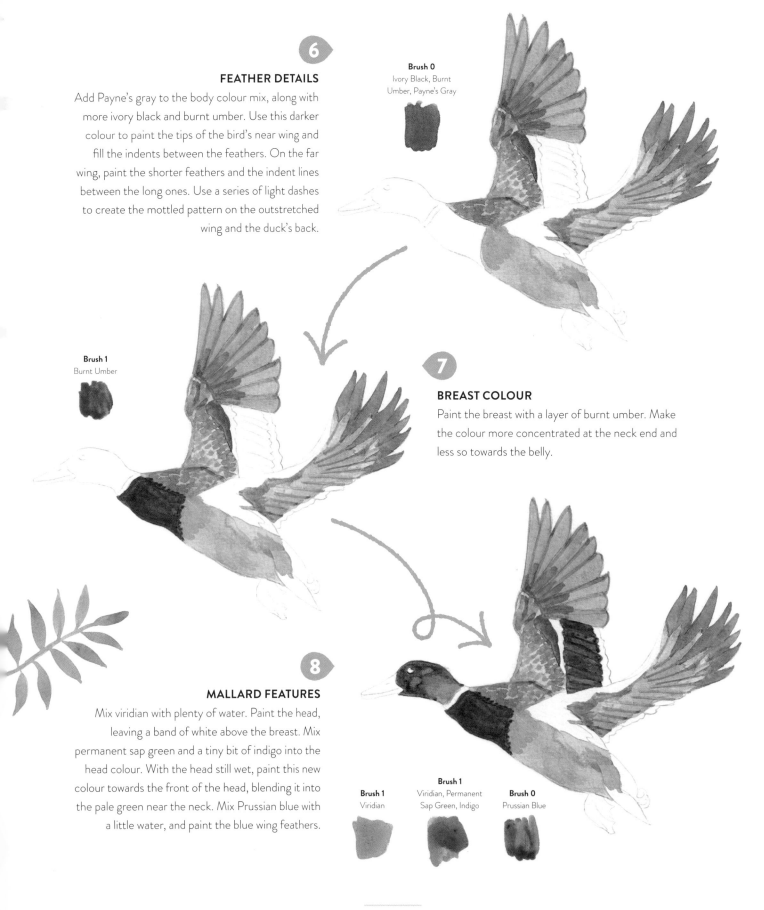

6

FEATHER DETAILS

Add Payne's gray to the body colour mix, along with more ivory black and burnt umber. Use this darker colour to paint the tips of the bird's near wing and fill the indents between the feathers. On the far wing, paint the shorter feathers and the indent lines between the long ones. Use a series of light dashes to create the mottled pattern on the outstretched wing and the duck's back.

Brush 0
Ivory Black, Burnt
Umber, Payne's Gray

Brush 1
Burnt Umber

7

BREAST COLOUR

Paint the breast with a layer of burnt umber. Make the colour more concentrated at the neck end and less so towards the belly.

8

MALLARD FEATURES

Mix viridian with plenty of water. Paint the head, leaving a band of white above the breast. Mix permanent sap green and a tiny bit of indigo into the head colour. With the head still wet, paint this new colour towards the front of the head, blending it into the pale green near the neck. Mix Prussian blue with a little water, and paint the blue wing feathers.

Brush 1
Viridian

Brush 1
Viridian, Permanent
Sap Green, Indigo

Brush 0
Prussian Blue

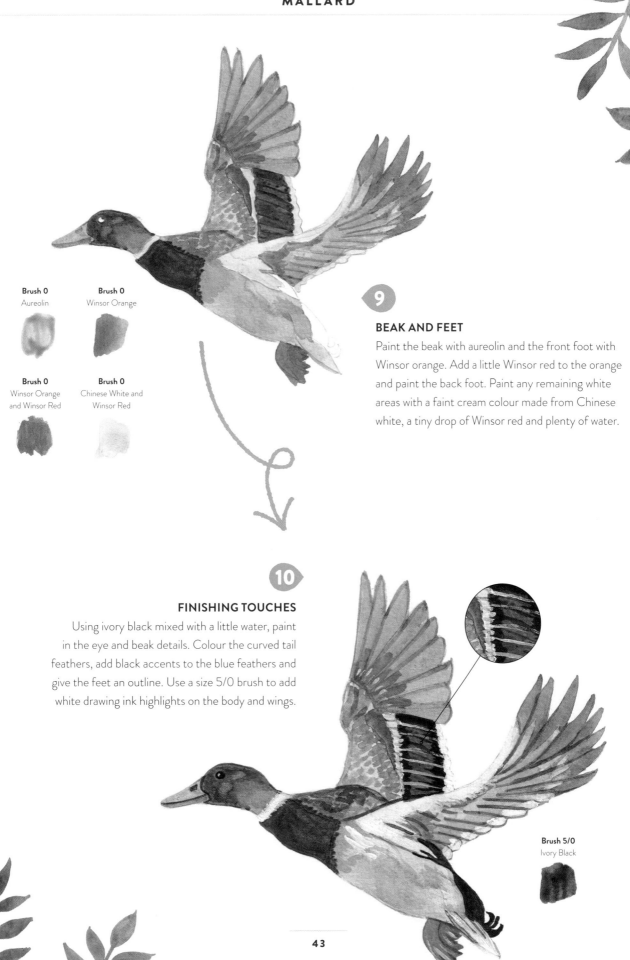

Brush 0
Aureolin

Brush 0
Winsor Orange

Brush 0
Winsor Orange
and Winsor Red

Brush 0
Chinese White and
Winsor Red

9

BEAK AND FEET

Paint the beak with aureolin and the front foot with Winsor orange. Add a little Winsor red to the orange and paint the back foot. Paint any remaining white areas with a faint cream colour made from Chinese white, a tiny drop of Winsor red and plenty of water.

10

FINISHING TOUCHES

Using ivory black mixed with a little water, paint in the eye and beak details. Colour the curved tail feathers, add black accents to the blue feathers and give the feet an outline. Use a size 5/0 brush to add white drawing ink highlights on the body and wings.

Brush 5/0
Ivory Black

GREY HERON

Ardea cinerea

Grey herons have rather simple colouring, but flashes of beautiful bright pink and yellow on the beak make the bird stand out.

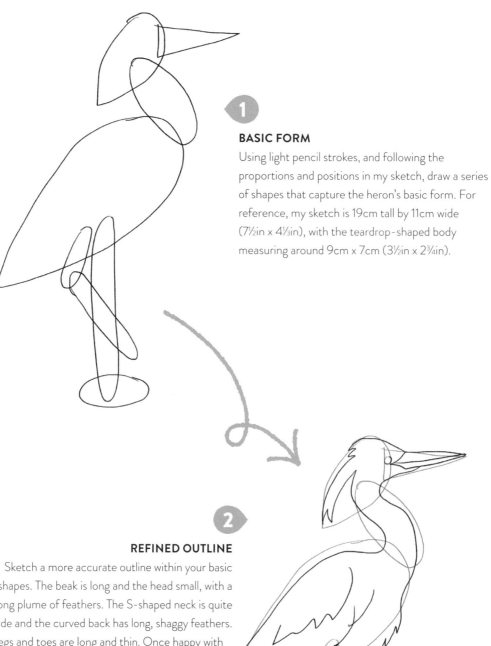

1

BASIC FORM

Using light pencil strokes, and following the proportions and positions in my sketch, draw a series of shapes that capture the heron's basic form. For reference, my sketch is 19cm tall by 11cm wide (7½in x 4⅓in), with the teardrop-shaped body measuring around 9cm x 7cm (3½in x 2¾in).

2

REFINED OUTLINE

Sketch a more accurate outline within your basic shapes. The beak is long and the head small, with a long plume of feathers. The S-shaped neck is quite wide and the curved back has long, shaggy feathers. Legs and toes are long and thin. Once happy with your outline, erase the basic shapes.

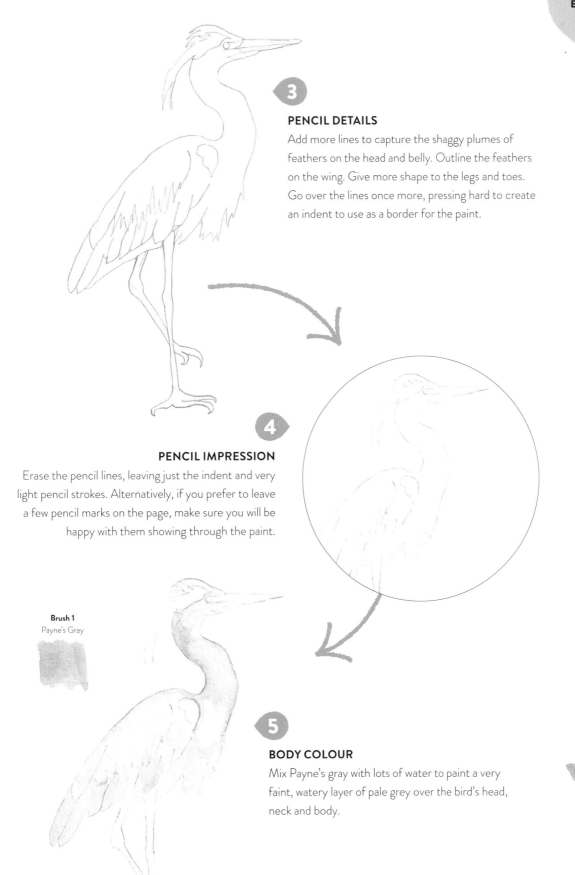

3

PENCIL DETAILS

Add more lines to capture the shaggy plumes of
feathers on the head and belly. Outline the feathers
on the wing. Give more shape to the legs and toes.
Go over the lines once more, pressing hard to create
an indent to use as a border for the paint.

4

PENCIL IMPRESSION

Erase the pencil lines, leaving just the indent and very
light pencil strokes. Alternatively, if you prefer to leave
a few pencil marks on the page, make sure you will be
happy with them showing through the paint.

Brush 1
Payne's Gray

5

BODY COLOUR

Mix Payne's gray with lots of water to paint a very
faint, watery layer of pale grey over the bird's head,
neck and body.

6

FEATHER DETAILS

Make a concentrated mix of Payne's gray to paint the heron's underbelly and the dark patch at the top of the wing. Add more water, and paint the small patch around the eye. Edge the front of the neck with this colour, blending it into the body colour. Paint long, fluid brushstrokes on the chest, wings and back to create layers of feathers.

Brush 1
Payne's Gray

Brush 1
Burnt Sienna

Brush 1
Burnt Sienna and
Permanent Alizarin Crimson

Brush 0
Ivory Black and Payne's Gray

7

LEGS AND HEAD

Paint the front leg and foot with a watery burnt sienna. Add more water and a little permanent alizarin crimson to the burnt sienna, and use this to paint the back leg, which is in shadow. Mix ivory black and Payne's gray with a little water to paint the feather plume on the head.

8

BEAK FEATURES

Using a concentrated aureolin mix, paint the eye and the tip of the beak. Mix permanent rose with a little water and paint this over the base of the beak, blending it into the wet yellow. When the paint is dry, add a thin line of Payne's gray down the middle of the beak.

Brush 000
Aureolin

Brush 000
Permanent Rose blended
with Aureolin

Brush 000
Payne's Gray

46

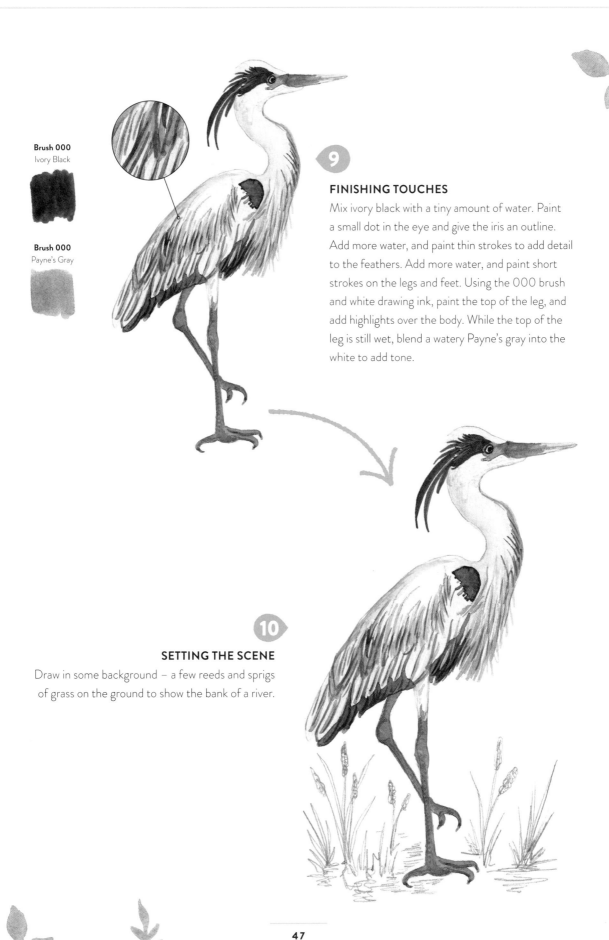

Brush 000
Ivory Black

Brush 000
Payne's Gray

9

FINISHING TOUCHES

Mix ivory black with a tiny amount of water. Paint a small dot in the eye and give the iris an outline. Add more water, and paint thin strokes to add detail to the feathers. Add more water, and paint short strokes on the legs and feet. Using the 000 brush and white drawing ink, paint the top of the leg, and add highlights over the body. While the top of the leg is still wet, blend a watery Payne's gray into the white to add tone.

10

SETTING THE SCENE

Draw in some background – a few reeds and sprigs of grass on the ground to show the bank of a river.

BLUE-AND-YELLOW MACAW

Ara ararauna

One of the most colourful projects in the book, this painting features a painted tree stump rather than a pencil drawing to set the scene.

Note how the elongated oval shape for the tail is slightly longer than the one for the body, measuring 12cm (4¾in).

1

BASIC FORM

Using light pencil strokes, and following the proportions and positions in my sketch, draw a series of shapes that capture the macaw's basic form. For reference, my sketch is 19cm tall by 7cm wide (7½in x 2¾in), with the body shape measuring 10cm (4in) long and the tail slightly longer, at 12cm (4¾in).

2

REFINED OUTLINE

Sketch a more accurate outline within your basic shapes. The head sits on a short neck, is almost flat on top and has a large, curved beak. The back follows the curve of the teardrop shape and the long tail has clearly defined feathers. The left foot is in the air and the right foot has its talons splayed. Once happy with your outline, erase the basic shapes.

PENCIL DETAILS

Using the final image as a reference, draw outlines for the different sections of colour and the macaw's facial features. Draw in the separate wing and tail feathers.

SETTING THE SCENE

Draw in a branch for the parrot to perch on, wrapping its right foot around the top of it. Go over your pencil lines once more, pressing hard to create an indent to use as a border for the paint.

PENCIL IMPRESSION

Erase the pencil lines, leaving just the indent and very light pencil strokes. Alternatively, if you prefer to leave a few pencil marks on the page, make sure you will be happy with them showing through the paint.

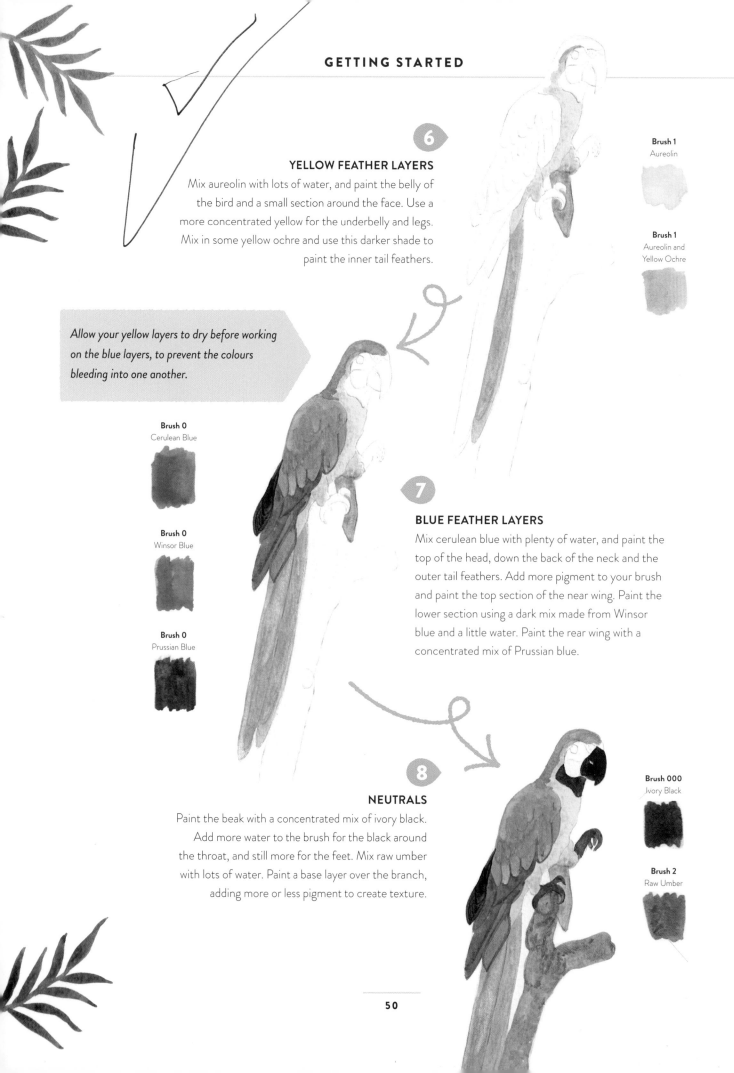

6

YELLOW FEATHER LAYERS

Mix aureolin with lots of water, and paint the belly of the bird and a small section around the face. Use a more concentrated yellow for the underbelly and legs. Mix in some yellow ochre and use this darker shade to paint the inner tail feathers.

Brush 1
Aureolin

Brush 1
Aureolin and
Yellow Ochre

Allow your yellow layers to dry before working on the blue layers, to prevent the colours bleeding into one another.

Brush 0
Cerulean Blue

Brush 0
Winsor Blue

Brush 0
Prussian Blue

7

BLUE FEATHER LAYERS

Mix cerulean blue with plenty of water, and paint the top of the head, down the back of the neck and the outer tail feathers. Add more pigment to your brush and paint the top section of the near wing. Paint the lower section using a dark mix made from Winsor blue and a little water. Paint the rear wing with a concentrated mix of Prussian blue.

8

NEUTRALS

Paint the beak with a concentrated mix of ivory black. Add more water to the brush for the black around the throat, and still more for the feet. Mix raw umber with lots of water. Paint a base layer over the branch, adding more or less pigment to create texture.

Brush 000
Ivory Black

Brush 2
Raw Umber

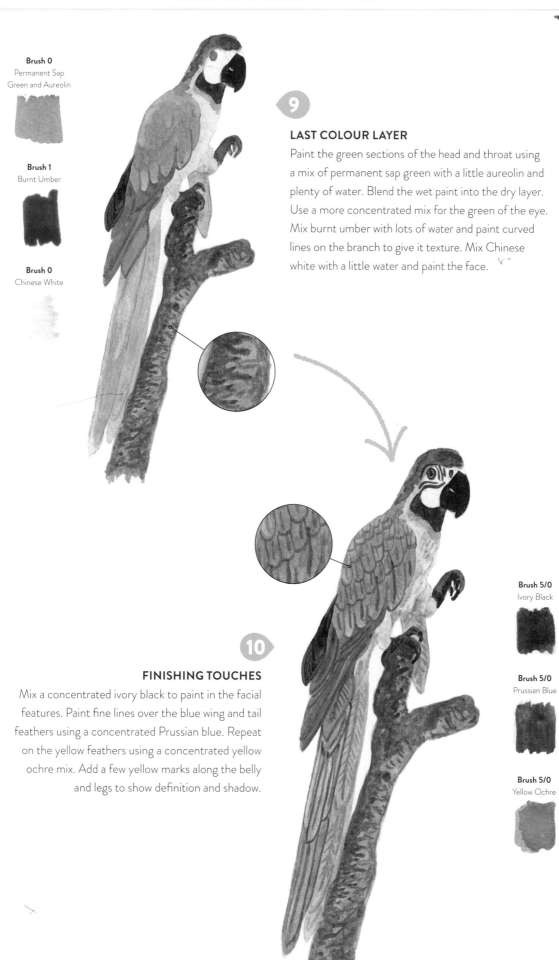

Brush 0
Permanent Sap
Green and Aureolin

Brush 1
Burnt Umber

Brush 0
Chinese White

9

LAST COLOUR LAYER

Paint the green sections of the head and throat using
a mix of permanent sap green with a little aureolin and
plenty of water. Blend the wet paint into the dry layer.
Use a more concentrated mix for the green of the eye.
Mix burnt umber with lots of water and paint curved
lines on the branch to give it texture. Mix Chinese
white with a little water and paint the face.

10

FINISHING TOUCHES

Mix a concentrated ivory black to paint in the facial
features. Paint fine lines over the blue wing and tail
feathers using a concentrated Prussian blue. Repeat
on the yellow feathers using a concentrated yellow
ochre mix. Add a few yellow marks along the belly
and legs to show definition and shadow.

Brush 5/0
Ivory Black

Brush 5/0
Prussian Blue

Brush 5/0
Yellow Ochre

BLACKBIRD

Turdus merula

The blackbird is common sight in British gardens. It can be tricky to show definition
when painting in just one colour, so here you will use a mix of browns and blacks to create tone.

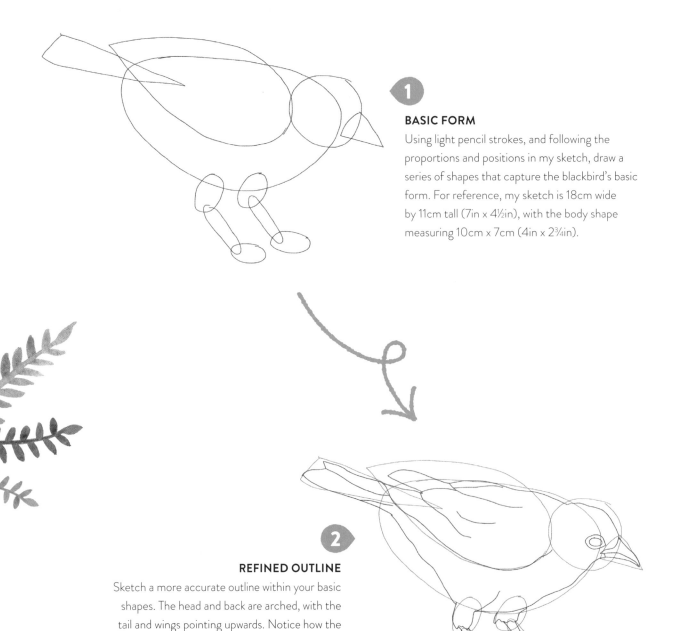

1

BASIC FORM

Using light pencil strokes, and following the
proportions and positions in my sketch, draw a
series of shapes that capture the blackbird's basic
form. For reference, my sketch is 18cm wide
by 11cm tall (7in x 4½in), with the body shape
measuring 10cm x 7cm (4in x 2¾in).

2

REFINED OUTLINE

Sketch a more accurate outline within your basic
shapes. The head and back are arched, with the
tail and wings pointing upwards. Notice how the
thin beak has a slight downward curve. The legs
are jointed and the feet are long and thin. Once
happy with your outline, erase the basic shapes.

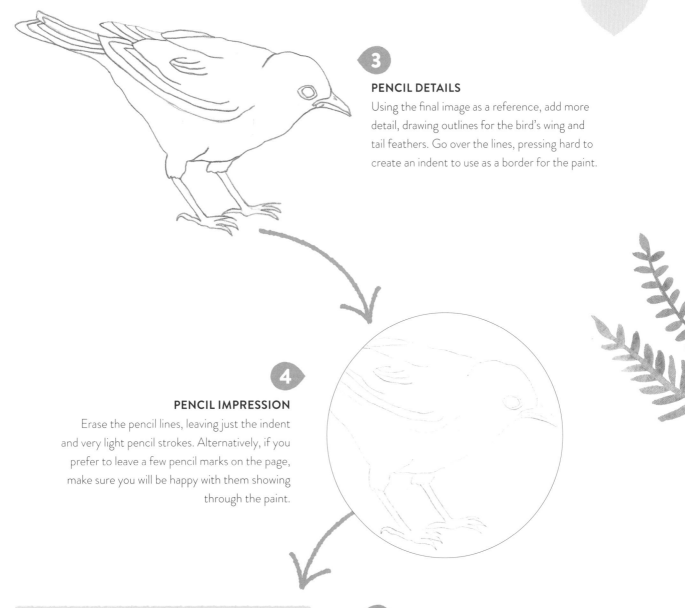

3

PENCIL DETAILS

Using the final image as a reference, add more detail, drawing outlines for the bird's wing and tail feathers. Go over the lines, pressing hard to create an indent to use as a border for the paint.

4

PENCIL IMPRESSION

Erase the pencil lines, leaving just the indent and very light pencil strokes. Alternatively, if you prefer to leave a few pencil marks on the page, make sure you will be happy with them showing through the paint.

Remember, if you apply too much paint, you can remove some by patting the area with a paper towel or by washing over the paint with a wet paintbrush.

5

BODY COLOUR

Mix burnt umber and ivory black with plenty of water. Paint long, sweeping strokes over the body, tail and wing. Add more or less pigment to create variation in this base layer. The colour should be fairly opaque, but still watery enough to see the indented pencil lines.

Brush 2
Burnt Umber
and Ivory Black

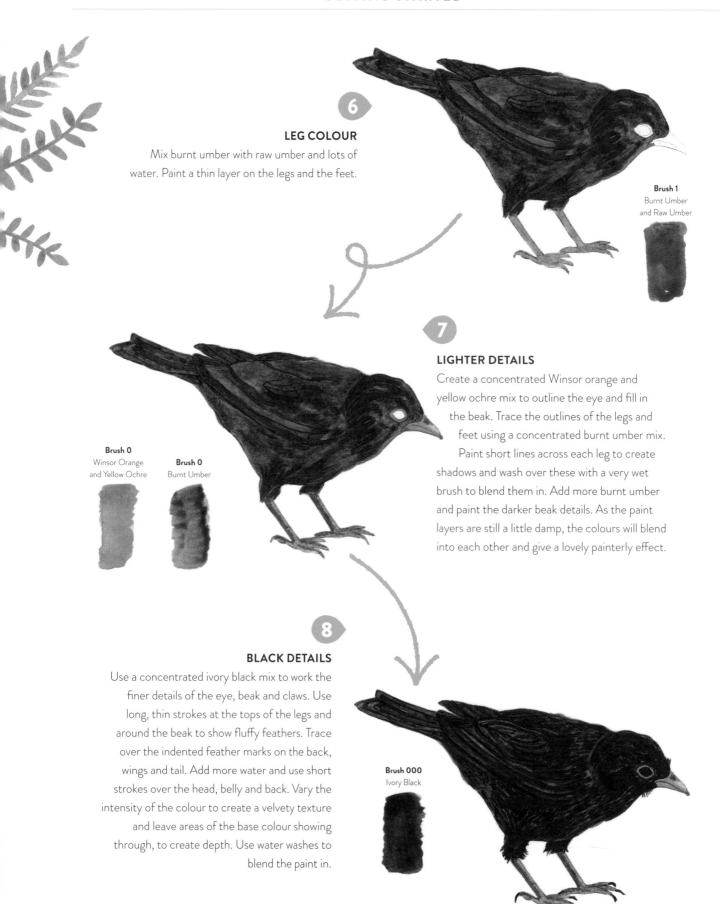

6

LEG COLOUR

Mix burnt umber with raw umber and lots of water. Paint a thin layer on the legs and the feet.

Brush 1
Burnt Umber and Raw Umber

Brush 0
Winsor Orange and Yellow Ochre

Brush 0
Burnt Umber

7

LIGHTER DETAILS

Create a concentrated Winsor orange and yellow ochre mix to outline the eye and fill in the beak. Trace the outlines of the legs and feet using a concentrated burnt umber mix. Paint short lines across each leg to create shadows and wash over these with a very wet brush to blend them in. Add more burnt umber and paint the darker beak details. As the paint layers are still a little damp, the colours will blend into each other and give a lovely painterly effect.

8

BLACK DETAILS

Use a concentrated ivory black mix to work the finer details of the eye, beak and claws. Use long, thin strokes at the tops of the legs and around the beak to show fluffy feathers. Trace over the indented feather marks on the back, wings and tail. Add more water and use short strokes over the head, belly and back. Vary the intensity of the colour to create a velvety texture and leave areas of the base colour showing through, to create depth. Use water washes to blend the paint in.

Brush 000
Ivory Black

9

SETTING THE SCENE

Using a pencil, sketch a background – scribble some lines to suggest the ground and a few tufts of grass. The lines should be fairly light and soft so as not to detract from the painting.

The white highlights are entirely optional – the bird is quite complete without them – but they will really make the details pop.

10

WHITE HIGHLIGHTS

Add some white drawing ink highlights using a 000 brush, starting with the light reflected in the bird's eye. Paint short strokes on the face, radiating away from the beak. Use the ink to highlight feather details on the wing and tail.

2

BUILDING CONFIDENCE

This selection of projects builds on what you have learned already, and introduces a few more complicated techniques. These birds have bright, colourful plumage and detailed markings. Much of the work involves building texture in layers of colour and adding fine white detail using small paintbrushes.

AMERICAN ROBIN

Turdus migratorius

Belonging to the same family as the blackbird, the American robin is a different species to the European robin, but shares its name due to its red breast.

1

BASIC FORM

Using light pencil strokes, and following the proportions and positions in my sketch, draw a series of shapes that capture the robin's basic form. For reference, my sketch is 13½cm tall by 16cm wide (5⅓in x 6¼in), with the oval breast shape measuring 9cm x 6cm (3½in x 2⅓in).

2

REFINED OUTLINE

Sketch a more accurate outline within your basic shapes. Note how small the head is in comparison to the rest of the body, with a fairly flat top. The long, thin wings and tail all point in the same downward direction. The large chest curves outwards from the neck. Add some quick lines around the eye and at the top of the chest to signify different sections of colour. Once happy with your outline, erase the basic shapes.

If adding a twig, as in Step 10, it could help to sketch it in at this stage, to take account of perspective.

PENCIL DETAILS

Using the final image as a reference, draw more detail, marking the layers of wing and tail feathers. Go over the lines once more, pressing hard to create an indent to use as a border for the paint.

PENCIL IMPRESSION

Erase the pencil lines, leaving just the indent and very light pencil strokes. Alternatively, if you prefer to leave a few pencil marks on the page, make sure you will be happy with them showing through the paint.

Brush 1
Yellow Ochre and
Winsor Orange

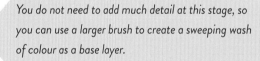

You do not need to add much detail at this stage, so you can use a larger brush to create a sweeping wash of colour as a base layer.

Brush 1
Yellow Ochre

BREAST AND BEAK

Mix yellow ochre and Winsor orange with plenty of water. Paint a watery layer over the breast. Vary the amounts of pigment and water to create texture, letting the colour bleed. Mix yellow ochre with a little water and paint a semi-opaque layer over the beak.

6 HEAD, WING AND TAIL

Mix Payne's gray and ivory black with lots of water, and use this to paint a watery layer over the head, wing and tail. Lighten the wing colour with a little more water.

Brush 1
Payne's Gray and Ivory Black

Brush 1
Burnt Umber

Brush 1
Burnt Sienna and Yellow Ochre

Brush 1
Chinese White

7 BUILDING COLOUR

Use concentrated mixes of the following: burnt umber for the legs and feet; and Chinese white for the eye patch and at the top of the leg. Add a tiny amount of Payne's gray to the white, and paint the underside of the tail and the small patch above the breast. Mix burnt sienna and yellow ochre to paint short, downward strokes on the robin's breast, making them more concentrated towards the legs.

8 TEXTURE AND HIGHLIGHTS

Create a concentrated mix of ivory black and Payne's gray. Following the curve of the robin's head, make a series of short strokes that radiate out from the beak and down to the breast. Brush water over the strokes to blend them in. Use the same mix to paint feather details on the wing and tail. Add lots more water and use this lighter colour to add texture to the white patches. Dab the paint with a paper towel while wet, to leave just a faint grey tone. Use a concentrated burnt umber mix to paint thin lines on the legs and feet.

Brush 1
Ivory Black and Payne's Gray

Brush 1
Burnt Umber

Brush 000
Ivory Black

Brush 0
Chinese White

⑨ FINISHING TOUCHES

Use a concentrated ivory black mix to fill in the eye and add a few darker lines on the head, wing and tail to bring out the highlights. Add a little water to the black and paint a thin line along the beak and where the leg joins the body. Dab these lines with a paper towel to soften the colour. Mix Chinese white with a little water and paint the patches around the eye and below the neck. Paint a few watery strokes over the head and breast.

⑩ SETTING THE SCENE

Draw some background detail for your bird – a twig and some sprigs of festive foliage. Use loose, scribbly marks to create texture on the twig and a series of short, scribbled lines for the greenery.

NORTHERN CARDINAL

Cardinalis cardinalis

This is a male cardinal. The males have beautiful bright-red markings, whereas the females are a much more muted brown in colour.

1

BASIC FORM

Using light pencil strokes, and following the proportions and positions in my sketch, draw a series of shapes that capture the cardinal's basic form. For reference, my sketch is 19cm tall by 12cm wide (7½in x 4¾in), with the oval body shape measuring 9cm x 8cm (3½in x 3in).

2

REFINED OUTLINE

Sketch a more accurate outline within your basic shapes, noting the curve of the beak and the feathers on the top of the bird's head. Define the black face and the long tail feathers. Once happy with your outline, erase your basic shapes.

If adding a twig, as in Step 10, it could help to sketch it in at this stage, to take account of perspective.

3

PENCIL DETAILS

Using the final image as a reference, draw more detail, using long lines to show the layered wing and tail feathers. Go over the lines, pressing hard to create an indent to use as a border for the paint.

4

PENCIL IMPRESSION

Erase the pencil lines, leaving just the indent and very light pencil strokes. If you prefer to leave a few pencil marks on the page, make sure you will be happy with them showing through the paint.

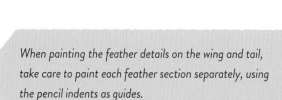

When painting the feather details on the wing and tail, take care to paint each feather section separately, using the pencil indents as guides.

Brush 1
Burnt Sienna, Winsor Red, Aureolin

Brush 1
Burnt Sienna, Winsor Red, Aureolin, Payne's Gray

5

BODY COLOUR

Mix burnt sienna, Winsor red and aureolin with plenty of water. Paint this all over the top of the head and the body, working in different directions to create texture. Add a tiny amount of Payne's gray to make brown and use this to paint the bird's wing and tail, and a tiny section above the eye. Add more or less water to create different tones.

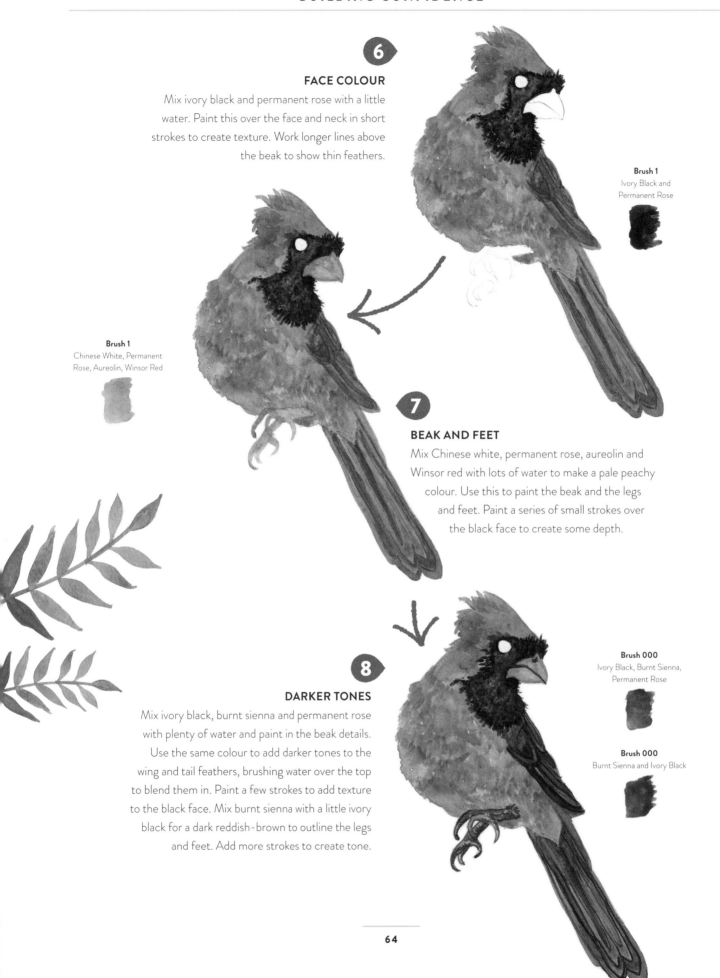

6

FACE COLOUR

Mix ivory black and permanent rose with a little water. Paint this over the face and neck in short strokes to create texture. Work longer lines above the beak to show thin feathers.

Brush 1
Ivory Black and Permanent Rose

Brush 1
Chinese White, Permanent Rose, Aureolin, Winsor Red

7

BEAK AND FEET

Mix Chinese white, permanent rose, aureolin and Winsor red with lots of water to make a pale peachy colour. Use this to paint the beak and the legs and feet. Paint a series of small strokes over the black face to create some depth.

Brush 000
Ivory Black, Burnt Sienna, Permanent Rose

8

DARKER TONES

Mix ivory black, burnt sienna and permanent rose with plenty of water and paint in the beak details. Use the same colour to add darker tones to the wing and tail feathers, brushing water over the top to blend them in. Paint a few strokes to add texture to the black face. Mix burnt sienna with a little ivory black for a dark reddish-brown to outline the legs and feet. Add more strokes to create tone.

Brush 000
Burnt Sienna and Ivory Black

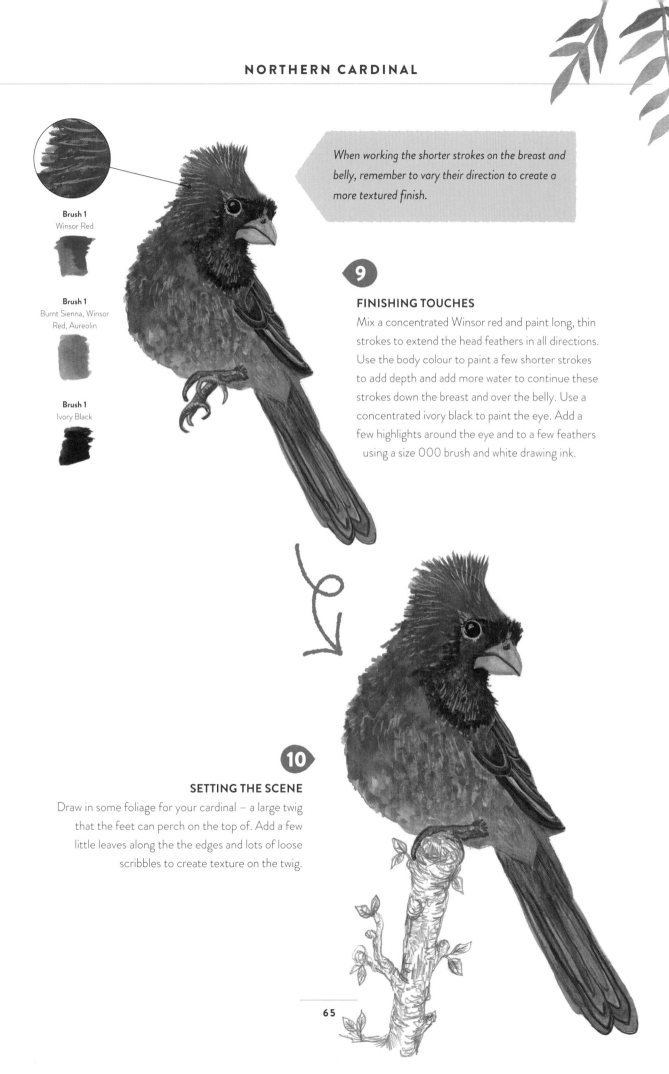

Brush 1
Winsor Red

Brush 1
Burnt Sienna, Winsor
Red, Aureolin

Brush 1
Ivory Black

When working the shorter strokes on the breast and belly, remember to vary their direction to create a more textured finish.

9

FINISHING TOUCHES

Mix a concentrated Winsor red and paint long, thin strokes to extend the head feathers in all directions. Use the body colour to paint a few shorter strokes to add depth and add more water to continue these strokes down the breast and over the belly. Use a concentrated ivory black to paint the eye. Add a few highlights around the eye and to a few feathers using a size 000 brush and white drawing ink.

10

SETTING THE SCENE

Draw in some foliage for your cardinal – a large twig that the feet can perch on the top of. Add a few little leaves along the the edges and lots of loose scribbles to create texture on the twig.

GOLDCREST
Regulus regulus

Dubbed a king among birds, the goldcrest has an olive-green body
and the male of the species has a beautiful bright stripe on his head.

1

BASIC FORM

Using light pencil strokes, and following the
proportions and positions in my sketch, draw
a series of shapes that capture the goldcrest's
basic form. For reference, my sketch is 17cm
wide by 13cm tall (6¾in x 5in), with the oval body
shape measuring 11cm x 9cm (4⅓in x 3½in).

*At only around 8.5cm (3½in) in length, the
goldcrest is Britain's smallest bird, making
my illustration larger than the real thing!*

*If adding twigs, as in Step 10, it could help to sketch
them in at this stage, to take account of perspective.*

2

REFINED OUTLINE

Sketch a more accurate outline within your
basic shapes. The body is round and the tufted
head doesn't extend far from the body. The feet
are thin and long, with splayed toes. Shape out
the folded wings and tail and draw in some light
feather details on the near wing. Once happy
with your outline, erase your basic shapes.

3

PENCIL DETAILS

Using the final image as a reference, draw more detail. Mark in the facial features and define the tufts on the head. Use long lines to draw in the layers of feathers on the wings and tail. Go over the lines once more, pressing hard to create an indent to use as a border for the paint.

4

PENCIL IMPRESSION

Erase the pencil lines, leaving just the indent and very light pencil strokes. Alternatively, if you prefer to leave a few pencil marks on the page, make sure you will be happy with them showing through the paint.

Brush 2
Winsor Yellow
and Olive Green

5

BODY COLOUR

Mix Winsor yellow and olive green with lots of water to paint a watery layer all over the body and head.

6

BUILDING COLOUR

Mix yellow ochre with lots of water to paint watery strokes over the head, chest and underbelly. Mix burnt umber with a little water to paint the legs and feet. Mix ivory black with a little water to paint the beak and a solid circle for the eye. Add some quick, long strokes to the tufts on top of the head.

Brush 2
Yellow Ochre

Brush 2
Burnt Umber

Brush 2
Ivory Black

7

BRIGHT FEATHERS

Mix olive green with a little water to paint the feathers at the top of the back. Mix aureolin and a little water to paint a few sections of the wings and tail, a patch on the bird's breast and the remaining tufts on the head. Mix burnt sienna with a little water and fill the inside of the mouth.

Brush 2
Olive Green

Brush 2
Aureolin

Brush 2
Burnt Sienna

8

BLACK AND WHITE ACCENTS

Mix ivory black and Payne's gray and use this to paint the remaining sections of the wings and the tail. Mix Chinese white with a little water and paint this around the eye, at the top of the wing and on the underbelly.

Brush 1
Ivory Black and
Payne's Gray

Brush 1
Chinese White

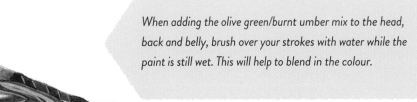

When adding the olive green/burnt umber mix to the head, back and belly, brush over your strokes with water while the paint is still wet. This will help to blend in the colour.

Brush 1
Olive Green and
Burnt Umber

Brush 000
Burnt Umber

9

TEXTURE AND TONE

Mix olive green and burnt umber with a little water and paint short strokes over the head, belly and back. Paint a thin layer of the same mix over the yellow on the wings and tail. Mix burnt umber with a little water to paint thin lines over the legs and to colour the tips of the toes. Still using a size 000 brush, add white drawing ink highlights to the head, around the eye and to the feathered sections of the wings and tail. Add a few short strokes on the underbelly, varying their direction.

10

SETTING THE SCENE

Draw a series of twigs and foliage sprigs for the bird to sit on. Fill in the twig outlines with a series of scribbled lines and hashes to create texture. Draw long strokes to create the leaves.

EURASIAN TREE SPARROW

Passer montanus

From afar, the sparrow looks mostly brown, but on approaching you can see the intricate patterns on the plumage, which you will pick out using a small paintbrush.

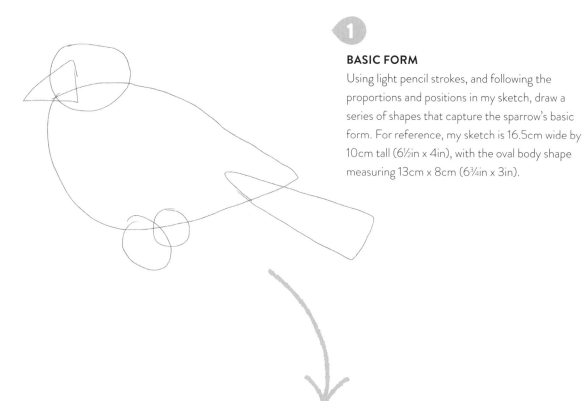

1 BASIC FORM

Using light pencil strokes, and following the proportions and positions in my sketch, draw a series of shapes that capture the sparrow's basic form. For reference, my sketch is 16.5cm wide by 10cm tall (6½in x 4in), with the oval body shape measuring 13cm x 8cm (6¾in x 3in).

If adding a twig, as in Step 10, it could help to sketch it in at this stage, to take account of perspective.

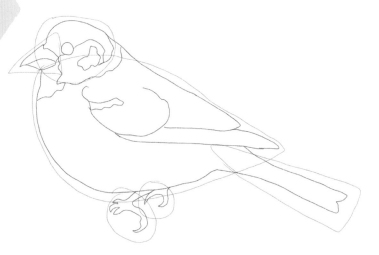

2 REFINED OUTLINE

Sketch a more accurate outline within your basic shapes. The head and back flow in a near-continuous line, and the tail and wings are pointing downwards. Notice how the beak is short, thick and downward-curving. The long, thin legs are hidden by the body and have curved toes. Once happy with your outline, erase your basic shapes.

The upper wings have an interesting pattern that looks as if it is made of lots of downward-pointing arrowheads.

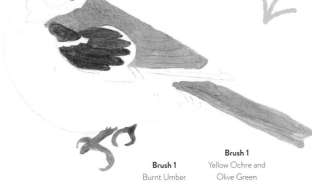

PENCIL DETAILS

Using the final image as a reference, draw more detail. Mark in the different sections of colour on the head, and the very detailed markings on the upper wings. Draw in the layers of feathers on the wings and tail. Go over the lines once more, pressing hard to create an indent to use as a border for the paint.

PENCIL IMPRESSION

Erase the pencil lines, leaving just the indent and very light pencil strokes. Alternatively, if you prefer to leave a few pencil marks on the page, make sure you will be happy with them showing through the paint.

BASE COLOURS

Mix burnt umber with a little water to create a semi-opaque colour for the top of the bird's head and a section of the wing. Add more water to the mix for the legs and feet. Mix yellow ochre and olive green with plenty of water to paint a watery base layer over the wings and tail.

Brush 1
Burnt Umber

Brush 1
Yellow Ochre and
Olive Green

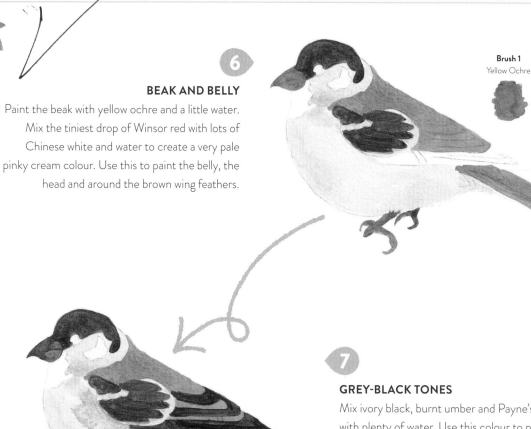

Brush 1
Yellow Ochre

Brush 2
Winsor Red and
Chinese White

6 BEAK AND BELLY

Paint the beak with yellow ochre and a little water.
Mix the tiniest drop of Winsor red with lots of
Chinese white and water to create a very pale
pinky cream colour. Use this to paint the belly, the
head and around the brown wing feathers.

7 GREY-BLACK TONES

Mix ivory black, burnt umber and Payne's gray
with plenty of water. Use this colour to paint
the darkest wing and tail feathers and the dark
beak details. Add lots more water to the
mix and paint where the belly meets the
wing. Lightly pad this with a paper towel to
create faint grey tones.

Brush 1
Ivory Black, Burnt
Umber, Payne's Gray

8 BROWN TONES

Mix burnt sienna and lots of water. Paint short
strokes over the head and the brown wing and tail
feathers. Switch to a size 0 brush to paint thin
lines at the rear edges of the legs and feet. Switch
back to the size 1 brush, add lots of water to the
mix and paint short, fat strokes over the belly area.
Dab with a paper towel so the paint is faint.

Brush 1 & 0
Burnt Sienna

9

FINISHING TOUCHES

Using a concentrated ivory black mix, paint the facial features – the bird's eye, the line down the middle of the beak, and the cheek and throat patches. Paint the claws at the ends of the toes. Paint the darkest tones on the wings and tail and the chevron shapes beneath the tail. Paint the highlight in the eye using a concentrated Chinese white.

Brush 000
Ivory Black

Brush 000
Chinese White

10

SETTING THE SCENE

Draw a twig for the bird to perch on. Using soft, quick lines, sketch out the rough outline and fill with scribbles to add texture.

BALD EAGLE

Haliaeetus leucocephalus

The emblem of the United States, and one of the country's largest birds of prey,
the bald eagle has a majestic wingspan of 200cm (80in).

1 BASIC FORM

Using light pencil strokes, and following the
proportions and positions in my sketch, draw a series
of shapes that capture the eagle's mid-flight form.
For reference, my sketch is 20cm wide by 11cm tall
(8in x 4⅓in), with the near wing, a teardrop shape,
measuring 11cm x 7cm (4⅓in x 2¾in).

2 REFINED OUTLINE

Sketch a more accurate outline within your basic
shapes. Note that the wings are angular, with multiple
feather sections. The head is arched with a curved
beak. The legs have full, fluffy feathers and the feet
have long talons. Once happy with your outline, erase
your basic shapes.

3

PENCIL DETAILS

Using the final image as a reference, add more detail. Draw long lines for the wing and tail feathers and outline the shaggy feathers on the legs and head. Go over the lines once more, pressing hard to create an indent to use as a border for the paint.

4

PENCIL IMPRESSION

Erase the pencil lines, leaving just the indent and very light pencil strokes. Alternatively, if you prefer to leave a few pencil marks on the page, make sure you will be happy with them showing through the paint.

5

BASE LAYERS

Mix ivory black and burnt umber with plenty of water. Paint this over the belly, the legs and the top of the wings. Add more ivory black to paint the tips of the wings and the longest feathers, painting each one separately between the indents.

Brush 2
Ivory Black and
Burnt Umber

Brush 2
Raw Umber and
Chinese White

6

TAIL FEATHERS

Add a tiny drop of raw umber to lots of Chinese white and water. Use this to paint alternate tail feathers and leave to dry. Add a little more raw umber to paint the remaining tail feathers.

7

HEAD COLOUR

Add more Chinese white and a drop of Payne's gray to the tail colour. Add lots more water and paint over the top of the head, leaving the eye and beak blank.

Brush 2
Raw Umber, Chinese
White, Payne's Gray

8

BUILDING TONE

Add another drop of Payne's gray and paint long streaks over the head. Blend them with water and dab with a paper towel if the colour looks too concentrated. Use the same colour to add tone to the tail feathers. Mix aureolin with a little water. Paint the beak and feet, adding more pigment for the darker areas. Add Chinese white to the mix to paint the eye.

Brush 1
Raw Umber, Chinese
White, Payne's Gray

Brush 1
Aureolin

Brush 0
Aureolin and
Chinese White

This is a project in which you work a large number of fine details into the last two layers.

Brush 1
Payne's Gray
and Burnt Umber

9 BUILDING TEXTURE

Mix Payne's gray and burnt umber with just a little water to make a concentrated dark brown. Use this colour to create texture by layering short, diagonal dashes on the wings and by stacking little scallop shapes on the body, making them more elongated on the legs. Give the legs a fluffy outline and paint long strokes where the tail joins the body.

10 FINISHING TOUCHES

Use a concentrated ivory black to paint the bird's talons and the fine details on the eye and beak – use a little water to blend in the patch around the eye. Add a few black lines radiating away from the eye and under the chin. Add more water to the brush to paint short strokes on the toes, dabbing them with a paper towel to knock back the colour. Still using a size 0 brush, use white drawing ink to add the highlights. Below the head, add a series of strokes graduating to a V on the chest. Paint a long stroke down each tail feather.

Brush 0
Ivory Black

RED JUNGLE FOWL

Gallus gallus

This tropical bird is known as the 'original chicken' and is much smaller than its domestic cousins. The male of the species has dramatic bursts of colourful plumage.

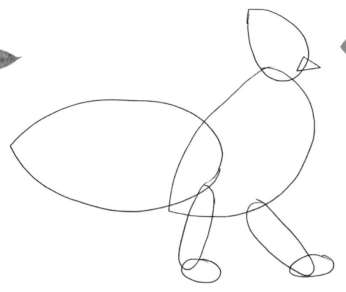

1 BASIC FORM

Using light pencil strokes, and following the proportions and positions in my sketch, draw a series of shapes that capture the bird's form. For reference, my sketch is 15cm wide by 13cm tall (6in x 5in), with the teardrop body shape measuring 9cm x 7cm (3½in x 2¾in).

2 REFINED OUTLINE

Sketch a more accurate outline within your basic shapes, starting with the plume of head feathers and the down-curved beak. Draw two shaggy shapes for the tops of the legs, and thin lower legs with wide feet. Add the layers of distinctive tail feathers. Once you have an outline you like, erase your basic shapes.

PENCIL DETAILS

Using the final image as a reference, add more detail. Add lines to mark the different sections of colour and the layers of feathers on the chest and the tail. Go over the lines, pressing hard to create an indent to use as a border for the paint.

PENCIL IMPRESSION

Erase the pencil lines, leaving just the indent and very light pencil strokes. Alternatively, if you prefer to leave a few pencil marks on the page, make sure you will be happy with them showing through the paint.

BLUE-GREEN TONES

Mix viridian, Winsor yellow and indigo with plenty of water and paint the bird's breast. While the paint is still wet, work quickly to create a watery Payne's gray and indigo mix. Mix this with a small amount of chest colour and paint from the legs upwards, blending the two colours where they meet. For the tail, follow the pencil indents to paint the lower half of each feather using this darker colour. Once these are dry paint the top half of each feather using the lighter mix.

Brush 2
Viridian, Winsor
Yellow, Indigo

Brush 2
Viridian, Winsor Yellow,
Indigo, Payne's Gray

Brush 2
Winsor Orange, Yellow
Ochre, Burnt Sienna

Brush 2
Winsor Orange, Yellow Ochre,
more Burnt Sienna

6

ORANGE-BROWN TONES

Mix equal parts of Winsor orange and yellow ochre. Add a drop of burnt sienna and plenty of wate to paint the top layer of feathers on the bird's face and back. Add more burnt sienna for the lower layers. Add more pigment to create the darkest areas. Use the very tip of your brush to paint the ends of the feathers.

7

BUILDING LAYERS

Mix burnt sienna and permanent alizarin crimson with plenty of water. Paint the face and the plume on top of the head. Add more crimson and, while the paint is still wet, repaint the plume to blend the colours. Paint this same dark red over the middle wing section. Mix a small amount of ivory black and Payne's gray with plenty of water to paint the legs and feet. Use the same colour to paint the beak, dabbing with a paper towel to remove excess pigment.

Brush 1
Burnt Sienna and
Permanent Alizarin Crimson

Brush 1
Ivory Black and
Payne's Gray

Brush 1
Cerulean Blue, Prussian
Blue, Viridian

Brush 1
Raw Umber

8

FINAL LAYERS

Mix cerulean blue, Prussian blue and viridian with plenty of water to fill in the final wing sections. Use a concentrated raw umber to paint the final body section.

9

FINER DETAILS

Paint the eye with a watery yellow ochre. Add more water and paint short strokes over the feathers on the back of the head and chest. Add Chinese white and more water to paint the remaining tail feathers. Clean the brush and paint the cheek patch using a concentrated Chinese white. Mix a very watery burnt sienna to paint thin, flowing lines over the orange section at the top of the back. Use a concentrated ivory black to paint the fine eye, beak and leg details. Mix permanent alizarin crimson with a little water to add highlights to the head plumage, face and middle wing section. Then mix Payne's gray with a little water to give the tail plumes their feathered edges. Add more water for the shaded tones on the cream tail feathers and the scalloped shapes on the bright blue wing sections.

Brush 1
Yellow Ochre

Brush 1
Chinese White
and Yellow Ochre

Brush 1
Chinese White

Brush 0
Burnt Sienna

Brush 5/0
Ivory Black

Brush 5/0
Permanent
Alizarin Crimson

Brush 5/0
Payne's Gray

I always leave the colours I've been using on my paint palette, so I can go back and 'reanimate' them at any time by adding more water. You never know when you might need that colour again, so don't wash it away until you're done painting!

10

FINISHING TOUCHES

Using a size 5/0 brush and white drawing ink, add short strokes over the head, chest and tail to show thin feathers. Lastly, set the scence for your bird, scribbling in some textured ground.

LONG-TAILED TIT

Aegithalos caudatus

This small garden bird is easily identified by its beautiful pale pink plumage, distinctive long tail and round body.

1 BASIC FORM

Using light pencil strokes, and following the proportions and positions in my sketch, draw a series of shapes that capture the bird's form. For reference, my sketch is 16cm wide by 11cm tall (6⅓in x 4⅓in), with the teardrop body shape measuring 10cm x 8.5cm (4in x 3⅓in).

2 REFINED OUTLINE

Sketch a more accurate outline within your shapes. There is a slight dip where the bird's head joins its back; the wings and tail point downwards. The feet are curved and have two long, pointed toes. Once happy with your outline, erase your basic shapes.

If adding a branch, as in Step 10, it could help to sketch it in at this stage, to take account of perspective.

3 PENCIL DETAILS

Using the final image as a reference, draw out different sections of colour. Note how the black of the back creeps into the face. Add the flash of pink along the top of the wing and draw long lines for the wing and tail feathers. Go over the lines, pressing hard to create an indent to use as a border for the paint.

4 PENCIL IMPRESSION

Erase the pencil lines, leaving just the indent and very light pencil strokes. Alternatively, if you prefer to leave a few pencil marks on the page, make sure you will be happy with them showing through the paint.

Remember, for the base layer you can make the first washes using a larger brush size and long, sweeping strokes.

Brush 2
Chinese White and
Permanent Rose

5 LIGHTER TONES

Mix Chinese white with a tiny drop of permanent rose and lots of water. Wash over the belly and the top of the head. Paint a thin layer over the top of the wings and along the lower edge of the tail.

6 DARKER TONES

Mix Payne's gray with ivory black and plenty of water and use this to create a watery wash over the top of the bird's head, back, wings and the upper tail feathers. Allow the paint to flow freely into the indented sections and use more or less water to vary the tone. Add burnt umber and a little water to the mix to create a deep, concentrated brown. Paint this over the feet and legs.

Brush 2
Payne's Gray
and Ivory Black

Brush 2
Payne's Gray, Ivory
Black, Burnt Umber

7

BUILDING THE PINKS

Mix permanent rose and raw sienna to make a watery orange-brown. Make short brushstrokes over the top of the wing and paint a small patch over the eye. Dab with a paper towel to create a soft texture. Add more water, and paint the underbelly, still dabbing with a paper towel. Add a little more pigment for where the underbelly joins the tail, to show shadow.

Brush 2
Permanent Rose
and Raw Sienna

If some sections look too concentrated, add just water to your brush and blend in the colour, dabbing with a paper towel if needed, to create a soft, blended edge.

8

DARKER DETAILS

Mix a concentrated ivory black to paint the beak, the eye and the shading on the legs and feet. Add a little more water to paint along the wing indents. On the black face patches, use short, thin strokes in varying directions to create the texture of short, fluffy feathers, blending them into the pink edges. Add more water to draw a thin line around the top of the head. Adding lots of water to the brush, paint a very watery grey layer where the underbelly meets the legs. Dab with a paper towel to remove any excess.

Brush 1
Ivory Black

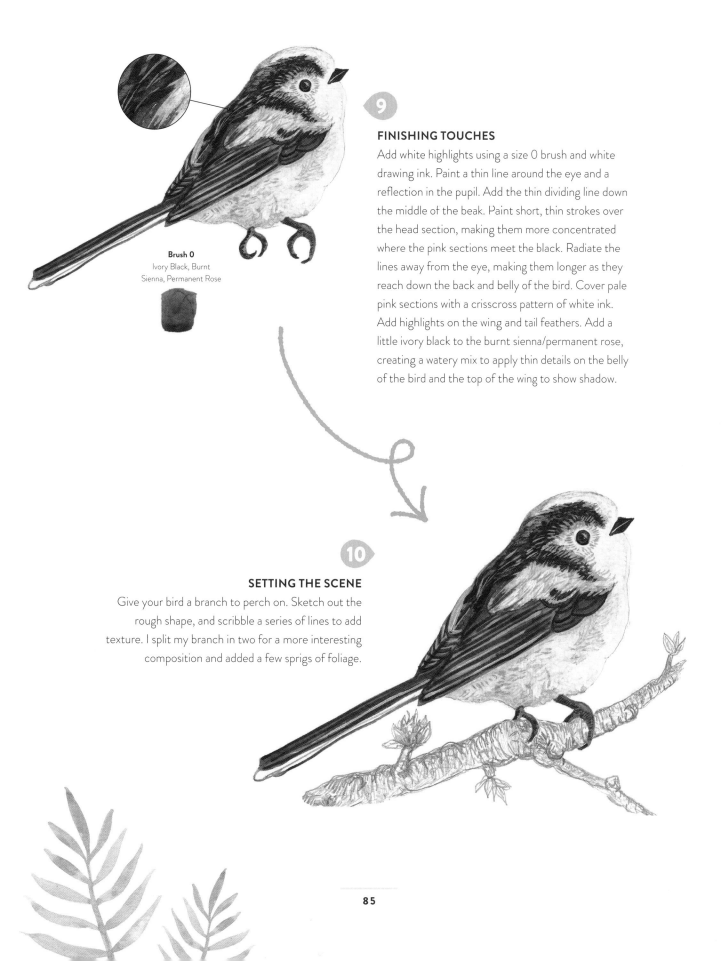

Brush 0
Ivory Black, Burnt
Sienna, Permanent Rose

9

FINISHING TOUCHES

Add white highlights using a size 0 brush and white drawing ink. Paint a thin line around the eye and a reflection in the pupil. Add the thin dividing line down the middle of the beak. Paint short, thin strokes over the head section, making them more concentrated where the pink sections meet the black. Radiate the lines away from the eye, making them longer as they reach down the back and belly of the bird. Cover pale pink sections with a crisscross pattern of white ink. Add highlights on the wing and tail feathers. Add a little ivory black to the burnt sienna/permanent rose, creating a watery mix to apply thin details on the belly of the bird and the top of the wing to show shadow.

10

SETTING THE SCENE

Give your bird a branch to perch on. Sketch out the rough shape, and scribble a series of lines to add texture. I split my branch in two for a more interesting composition and added a few sprigs of foliage.

PIGEON

Columba livia domestica

The pigeon is a common sight in urban areas. Its beautiful iridescent head and neck feathers contrast with the grey of its body and wings.

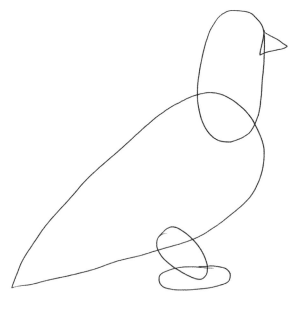

BASIC FORM

Using light pencil strokes, and following the proportions and positions in my sketch, draw a series of shapes that capture the pigeon's form. For reference, my sketch is 13cm wide by 13cm tall (5in x 5in), with the teardrop body shape measuring 10cm x 7cm (4in x 2¾in).

REFINED OUTLINE

Sketch a more accurate outline within your shapes. Note the bird's rounded head, long neck and gently undulating back. The chest is full and rounded. The short, stubby legs have long, thin feet with curved claws. Mark the separate wing and tail sections and add a few facial features. Once happy with your outline, erase your basic shapes.

PENCIL DETAILS

Using the final image as a reference, draw out different areas of colour. Mark the small raised section above the beak and add some lines to separate the feathers on the wings and the tail. Go over the lines once more, pressing hard to create an indent to use as a border for the paint.

PENCIL IMPRESSION

Erase the pencil lines, leaving just the indent and very light pencil strokes. Alternatively, if you prefer to leave a few pencil marks on the page, make sure you will be happy with them showing through the paint.

Brush 2
Payne's Gray and
Raw Sienna

DARK BASE COLOUR

Mix Payne's gray with a small amount of raw sienna and lots of water to create a watery ash colour. Use this to paint the head and tail sections and the darker sections of the wing feathers.

LIGHT BASE COLOUR

Add Chinese white and plenty of water to the dark base colour, to make a softer grey for the rest of the bird. Add more pigment to the brush to show the rear leg is in shadow. Mix a little raw sienna and permanent rose with plenty of water and use this for the feet. Add a drop more permanent rose for the shaded rear foot.

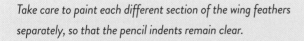

Take care to paint each different section of the wing feathers separately, so that the pencil indents remain clear.

Brush 2
Payne's Gray, Raw
Sienna, Chinese White

Brush 1
Raw Sienna and
Permanent Rose

7

IRIDESCENT NECK

To create the pigeon's iridescence, you need to work quickly, wet-on-wet. Paint a thin layer of water over the neck. Starting at the top with a band of quite concentrated aureolin, dab the paint onto the watery layer and watch the colour blend down. Add a viridian band, just below the aureolin. Keep adding water to the brush to allow the colours to blend smoothly. At the bottom of the neck, paint a concentrated indigo. Add more water to the brush and blend the colour upwards into the viridian. Dab the paint with a paper towel if the colour looks too concentrated.

Brush 2
Aureolin

Brush 2 Viridian

Brush 2
Indigo

Make sure this layer is completely dry before moving on. This might take longer than usual, because it uses so much water.

8

FEET AND FACIAL FEATURES

Mix burnt sienna and Winsor orange with a little water to paint the eye. Add some permanent rose to the mix, and use just the tip of the brush to paint a series of small lines along the edges of the feet to give them more shape. Mix a concentrated ivory black. Fill the beak and paint a thin line beneath the patch above it. Add a small black pupil and outline the iris.

Brush 1
Burnt Sienna and
Winsor Orange

Brush 1
Raw Sienna, Winsor Orange,
Permanent Rose

Brush 1
Ivory Black

Brush 0
Ivory Black, Payne's
Gray, Raw Sienna

Brush 0
Ivory Black

9

FINER DETAILS

Mix ivory black, Payne's gray and raw sienna with plenty of water to create a deep blue-green, and paint a series of watery dashes over the face and neck, radiating out from the eye. Give the white patch above the beak a thin top line. Trace the paint indents on the wing and tail feathers. Keep the paint watery and add more pigment for the darker feathers. Add more water to the mix and paint feathery details along the underbelly and legs. Paint a series of scallop shapes at the top of the wings. Use ivory black with a little water to paint a layer over the two dark strips on the wings.

10

FINISHING TOUCHES

Use a size 0 brush and white drawing ink to finish your painting. Paint over the white section above the beak and add a thin line along the middle of the beak. Add a highlight to the eye and series of fine lines radiating out below it. With quite a dry brush, paint long lines down the iridescent neck and pick out the curve of the breast just above the wing. I've also added a few lines along the front foot and leg. Draw in some background for the bird. As pigeons are often urban birds, I've drawn some rough pencil lines to indicate an asphalt ground.

GREAT TIT

Parus major

A common British garden visitor, this small, colourful bird is larger than the common blue tit, and can be distinguished by its black head and stripe down the breast.

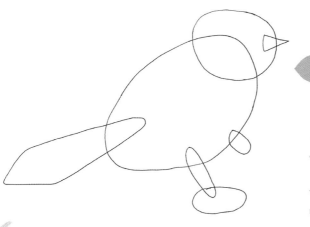

1 BASIC FORM

Using light pencil strokes, and following the proportions and positions in my sketch, draw a series of shapes that capture the bird's form. For reference, my sketch is 15cm wide by 12cm tall (6in x 4¾in), with the oval body shape measuring 9cm x 8cm (3½in x 3in).

2 REFINED OUTLINE

Sketch a more accurate outline within your shapes. Notice how chubby the belly is and how the head is almost square. Add a few lines to separate areas of colour. Once happy with your outline, erase your basic shapes.

If adding a branch, as in Step 10, it could help to sketch it in at this stage, to take account of perspective.

3 PENCIL DETAILS

Using the final image as a reference, add lines on the wing and tail to show the sections of feathers. Go over the lines once more, pressing hard to create an indent to use as a border for the paint.

4

PENCIL IMPRESSION

Erase the pencil lines, leaving just the indent and very light pencil strokes. Alternatively, if you prefer to leave the pencil marks on the page, make sure you will be happy with them showing through the paint.

Brush 1
Aureolin and
Lemon Yellow

Brush 1
Lemon Yellow and
Chinese White

Brush 1
Olive Green
and Sap Green

5

BASE COLOURS

Mix aureolin and lemon yellow with plenty of water to paint a base layer on the belly. Mix Chinese white with lemon yellow and water for the face and tail patches. Mix a more concentrated olive green and sap green mix for the upper back.

These layers will be built upon, so they don't need to be neat or solid – other layers will be added on top.

Brush 1 & 000
Ivory Black and Payne's Gray

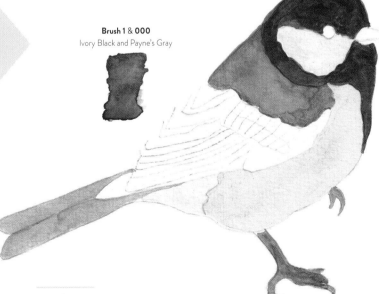

6

BASE GREYS

Mix ivory black and Payne's gray with a little water for concentrated colour. Paint a thin layer over the back of the head and under the beak. Add more water to paint a thin, lighter layer over the tail. Use the size 000 brush to paint this lighter colour on the legs and feet.

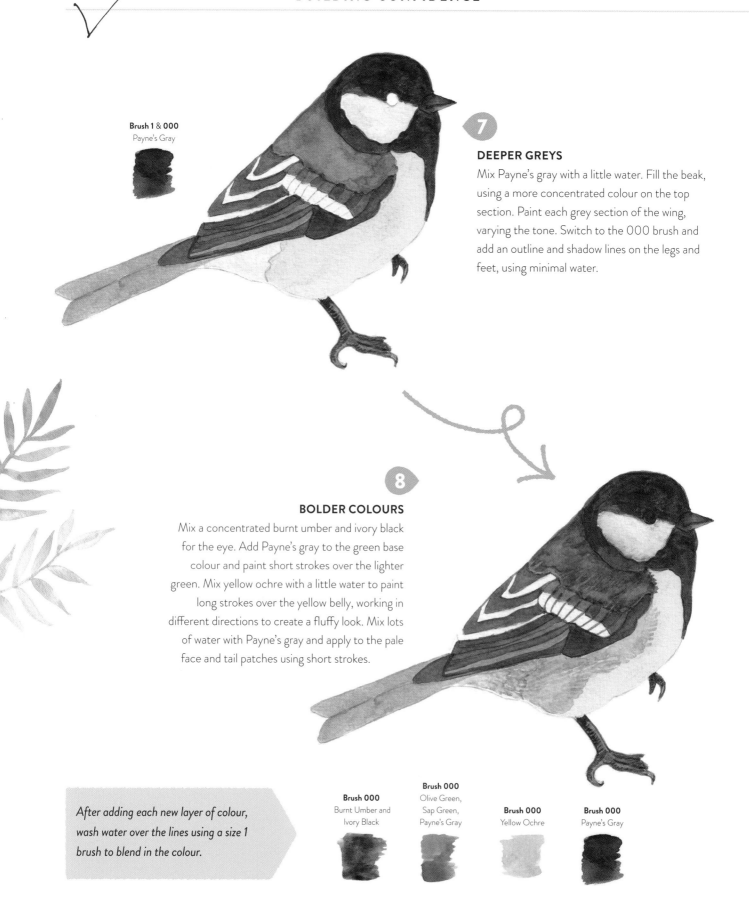

Brush 1 & 000
Payne's Gray

7

DEEPER GREYS

Mix Payne's gray with a little water. Fill the beak, using a more concentrated colour on the top section. Paint each grey section of the wing, varying the tone. Switch to the 000 brush and add an outline and shadow lines on the legs and feet, using minimal water.

8

BOLDER COLOURS

Mix a concentrated burnt umber and ivory black for the eye. Add Payne's gray to the green base colour and paint short strokes over the lighter green. Mix yellow ochre with a little water to paint long strokes over the yellow belly, working in different directions to create a fluffy look. Mix lots of water with Payne's gray and apply to the pale face and tail patches using short strokes.

After adding each new layer of colour, wash water over the lines using a size 1 brush to blend in the colour.

Brush 000
Burnt Umber and
Ivory Black

Brush 000
Olive Green,
Sap Green,
Payne's Gray

Brush 000
Yellow Ochre

Brush 000
Payne's Gray

Brush 000, 1 & 5/0
Ivory Black and Payne's Gray

9 DARK OUTLINES

Mix ivory black and Payne's gray with a little water, then brush long strokes down and around the tail. Add small strokes that follow the curves of the black head and belly areas to create texture. Use the size 1 brush to wash water over the strokes to blend them in. With water on your brush, trace around the lines on the wing. Mix a concentrated ivory black and use the size 5/0 brush to outline the brown eye. Draw a darker black circle within the brown eye.

10 PALE HIGHLIGHTS

Use a size 5/0 brush to add white drawing ink highlights in and around the eye and on the light face and tail patches. Add lines to divide the beak and give it an outline. Add a few highlights to the breast and underbelly and paint over the white details on the wing and tail. Finally, sketch in a pencil branch for your bird to perch on.

3

MASTERING
THE ART

Rise to the challenge of mastering a range of flying poses and detailed feather structures on outstretched wings. In this chapter, the pencil work at the start of each project requires more intricate detail, after which you will use what you have learned to build complex paint layers to create more accomplished pieces.

AMERICAN KESTREL

Falco sparverius

The American kestrel is the smallest falcon in North America.
It has beautiful patterning in its plumage, allowing for plenty of fine detail.

> *When capturing the kestrel's basic shape, note that the bird is flying at an angle.*

1 **BASIC FORM**

Using light pencil strokes, and following the proportions
and positions in my sketch, draw a series of shapes that
capture the kestrel's mid-flight form. For reference, my
sketch is 20cm wide by 12cm tall (8in x 4¾in), with the
near wing shape measuring 10cm x 5cm (4in x 2in).

2 **REFINED OUTLINE**

Sketch a more accurate outline within your basic shapes.
Notice how long and thin the wings are and how these
and the tail curve downwards. Capture the turn of the
bird's head and add a few facial features. Once you have
an outline you like, erase your basic shapes.

3 PENCIL DETAILS

Using the final image as a reference, draw out different sections of colour. Use long, sweeping lines to draw the feather details on the wings, making sure they follow the curve of the wing. Go over the lines once more, pressing hard to create an indent to use as a border for the paint.

4 PENCIL IMPRESSION

Erase the pencil lines, leaving just the indent and very light pencil strokes. Alternatively, if you prefer to leave a few pencil marks on the page, make sure you will be happy with them showing through the paint.

5 BASE COLOURS

Use Payne's gray with lots of water to apply a thin layer over the top section of the near wing, the top of the head, and the top and tips of the far wing. Add more pigment for the darker shades. Mix burnt sienna with plenty of water and, beside it on the palette, mix yellow ochre with plenty of water. Paint the top half of the bird's body with burnt sienna. While the paint is still wet, use yellow ochre to paint the bottom half of the body and into the tail. Let the two colours bleed into each other where they meet.

Brush 2
Payne's Gray

Brush 2
Burnt Sienna

Brush 2
Yellow Ochre

6
DARKER GREYS

Make an opaque ivory black and Payne's gray mix and paint alternate feathers on the lower section of the near wing. When dry, add more water to the mix and paint the remaining sections. Paint the grey sections of the tail feathers and the triangular patch where the body meets the tail. Use an even more concentrated mix to paint the underside of the far wing where it is cast in shadow.

Brush 1
Ivory Black and Payne's Gray

Brush 0
Burnt Umber

7
BODY MARKINGS

Mix burnt umber with a little water. Paint a small patch at the top of the head, then paint small, short strokes over the brown body, with the strokes getting longer as they reach the tail.

8
FACIAL FEATURES

Mix aureolin and a little water to paint the beak with a concentrated layer. Mix a tiny amount of Payne's gray with lots of Chinese white and a little water. Paint this around the eyes, on the top strip of the far wing and the lighter sections of the tail.

Brush 5/0
Aureolin

Brush 1
Payne's Gray and Chinese White

This pattern should look similar to a tiger's stripes.

Brush 000
Ivory Black

9

DETAILED MARKINGS

Using ivory black and a little water, add the finer details of the bird's markings. Fill the eyes and the tip of the beak. Add a little more water to the brush and add the dark facial features. Add black markings to the body, varying their size to emphasize its curves. Paint the very tips of the largest wing feathers and add oval markings and dashes on the smaller wing feathers. Paint chevrons on the underside of the far wing. Trace the outlines of the tail feathers and add the small strips of black close to where the tail meets the body.

10

WHITE HIGHLIGHTS

Apply the last details using a size 5/0 brush and white drawing ink. On the near wing, paint white ovals on the largest feathers. At the tops of these feathers trace the outlines of the sections above. Add a few highlights to the brown section of the tail. Pick out the reflection of light in the eyes and outline the irises. Trace the curve of the far wing, starting on the top and continuing on the underside, to capture the movement of the bird. Add highlights to the underside of the feathers on the far wing.

BARN OWL

Tyto alba

The undersides of the barn owl's wings are pale but become almost translucent in flight, allowing the beautiful markings of the top feathers to show through.

When capturing the barn owl's basic shape, note that the bird is flying at an angle.

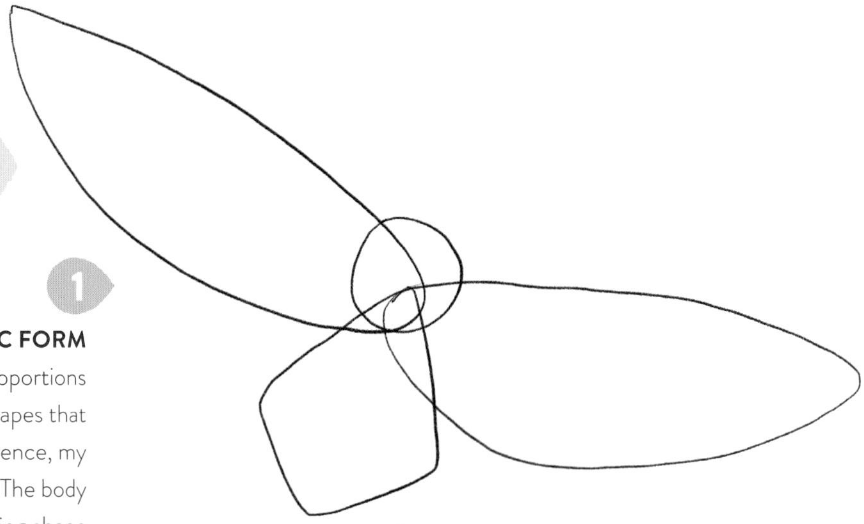

1

BASIC FORM

Using light pencil strokes, and following the proportions and positions in my sketch, draw a series of shapes that capture the owl's mid-flight form. For reference, my sketch is 20cm wide by 6cm tall (8in x 2⅓in). The body measures 6cm x 3cm (2⅓in x 1¼in) and each wing shape 9cm x 4cm (3⅔in x 1⅔in).

2

REFINED OUTLINE

Sketch a more accurate outline within your shapes. Notice how small the owl's body is, its very round head and its little, dangling legs. Draw in the feather sections. Once happy with your outline, erase your basic shapes.

3

PENCIL DETAILS

Using the final image as a reference, draw out different sections of colour. Mark the feather details on the wings, drawing long sweeping lines that follow the curve of the wing. Go over the lines once more, pressing hard to create an indent to use as a border for the paint.

4

PENCIL IMPRESSION

Erase the pencil lines, leaving just the indent and very light pencil strokes. Alternatively, if you prefer to leave a few pencil marks on the page, make sure you will be happy with them showing through the paint.

Your work doesn't need to be neat or even at this stage, and it doesn't matter if you can see the pencil lines showing through.

Brush 2
Yellow Ochre and
Lemon Yellow

5

BASE COLOUR

Using lots of water, mix yellow ochre and lemon yellow to create a watery light brown. Paint a thin wash of this all over the bird (apart from the eyes).

6

UPPER WINGS AND BODY

Mix raw sienna with lots of water and apply a thin layer over the owl's head and body. Continue over the upper sections of the outstretched wings.

Brush 2
Raw Sienna

Brush 2
Payne's Gray

7

GREY TONES

Mix Payne's gray with lots of water and paint short strokes around the eyes. Add more water and paint over the legs and lower half of the body. Add more water and paint short strokes midway up the lower wing sections.

8

BUILDING COLOUR

Mix burnt umber with lots of water and paint short strokes on the head and around and between the two eyes to frame them. Paint a small V for the beak. Paint a thin layer of the same colour along the tops of the wings and on the belly. Paint the very tips of the feathers on the wings and tail. Mix ivory black with a little water and paint a circle for each eye.

Brush 0
Burnt Umber

Brush 000
Ivory Black

Brush 0
Ivory Black

Brush 0
Burnt Umber

Brush 0
Raw Sienna

9 DETAILED MARKINGS

Mix ivory black with lots of water and paint rough-edged dots on the lower wing and tail sections. Use the same colour to trace the edge of each feather indent. Mix a concentrated burnt umber colour and paint small, short strokes on the darker areas of the upper wing sections and below the face. Mix raw sienna with a little water and paint short strokes on the lighter areas of the upper wing sections. Add more water to this colour and dab a few strokes over the grey patches on the face.

When adding highlights, remember that you can easily use the Chinese white watercolour block with only a little water to achieve the same effects as the white drawing ink.

10 WHITE HIGHLIGHTS

Using a size 000 brush and white drawing ink, trace around each eye and add the reflected light in the pupils. Paint small lines around the eyes and beak and circling the face. On the darkest areas, paint a series of small dashes to create a pebbled effect. Paint a long thin line down the centre of each of the longest wing feathers and the tail feathers. Add a few highlights in the lightest areas.

EURASIAN BULLFINCH

Pyrrhula pyrrhula

The male bullfinch is unmistakable, with his bright pinkish-red breast and cheeks.
Bullfinches can be seen in woodlands, orchards and hedgerows.

BASIC FORM

Using light pencil strokes, and following the proportions and positions in my sketch, draw a series of shapes that capture the bird's form. For reference, my sketch is 13cm wide by 12cm tall (5in x 4¾in), with the oval body shape measuring 9cm x 8cm (3½in x 3in).

REFINED OUTLINE

Sketch a more accurate outline within your basic shapes. Notice how the back of the bird's head doesn't curve in at the nape. The beak is curved downward and the ends of the tail and wings are rounded rather than pointy. Once you have an outline you like, erase your basic shapes.

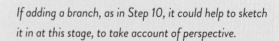

If adding a branch, as in Step 10, it could help to sketch it in at this stage, to take account of perspective.

PENCIL DETAILS

Using the final image as a reference, draw out the different markings on the wings, the claws and lines to distinguish different areas of colour. Go over the lines once more, pressing hard to create an indent to use as a border for the paint.

PENCIL IMPRESSION

Erase the pencil lines, leaving just the indent and very light pencil strokes. Alternatively, if you prefer to leave a few pencil marks on the page, make sure you will be happy with them showing through the paint.

Brush 2
Burnt Sienna and
Winsor Red

BASE LAYER

Using plenty of water, mix burnt sienna and Winsor red to make a deep red colour. Spread the paint across the water on the belly until it fills the space. Also add a small section of this red to the tips of the wings.

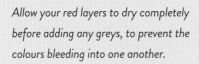

Allow your red layers to dry completely before adding any greys, to prevent the colours bleeding into one another.

GREY TONES

Add a little Payne's gray to Chinese white. Spread a small amount of water on the back of the bird and the underbelly, then add the soft grey mix. The paint should fill the area but needs to be quite watery. Paint the beak grey, too.

Brush 2
Payne's Gray and
Chinese White

Brush 1
Ivory Black and
Payne's Gray

7

BUILDING THE GREYS

Mix a concentrated ivory black and Payne's gray and carefully paint the eye and beak details. Add more water and paint the head, leaving a white outline around the eye. Paint the tail, using long brushstrokes, in an upward direction. Following the indents, paint the darkest wing feathers, varying the amount of water you use to create a striped effect. At the top of the wing, blend the black into the grey.

8

BUILDING COLOUR

Mix raw sienna and yellow ochre to make a sandy colour for the legs. While the paint is still wet, mix in some dark brown along the edges of the legs, made by adding a little ivory black to burnt umber. Add more water to the leg colour and paint small brushstrokes along the underbelly and at the top of the breast. Paint the blank areas on the wing with a concentrated Chinese white.

Brush 1
Raw Sienna and
Yellow Ochre

Brush 1
Burnt Umber
and Ivory Black

Brush 1
Chinese White

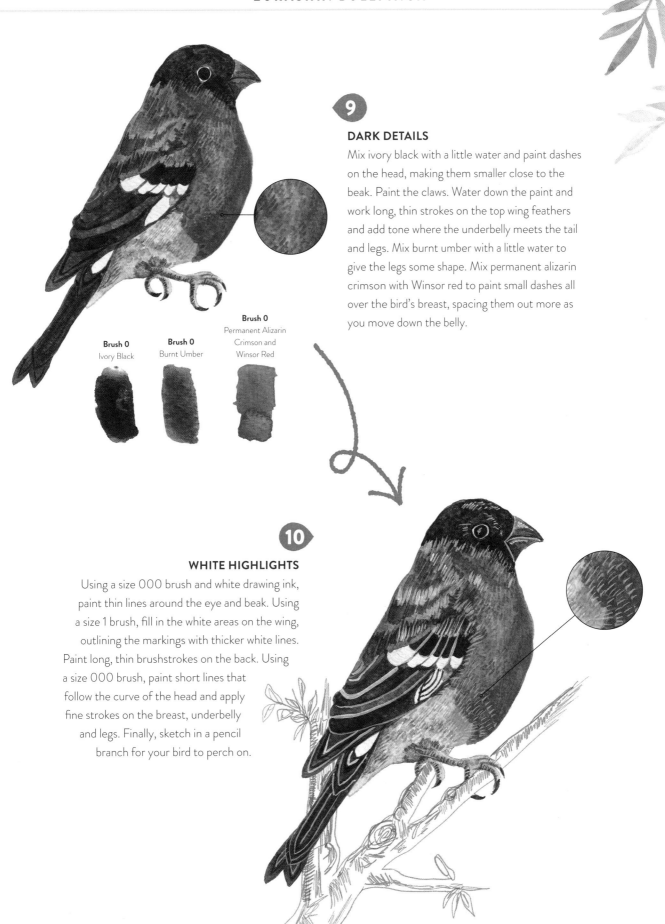

9

DARK DETAILS

Mix ivory black with a little water and paint dashes on the head, making them smaller close to the beak. Paint the claws. Water down the paint and work long, thin strokes on the top wing feathers and add tone where the underbelly meets the tail and legs. Mix burnt umber with a little water to give the legs some shape. Mix permanent alizarin crimson with Winsor red to paint small dashes all over the bird's breast, spacing them out more as you move down the belly.

Brush 0
Ivory Black

Brush 0
Burnt Umber

Brush 0
Permanent Alizarin
Crimson and
Winsor Red

10

WHITE HIGHLIGHTS

Using a size 000 brush and white drawing ink, paint thin lines around the eye and beak. Using a size 1 brush, fill in the white areas on the wing, outlining the markings with thicker white lines. Paint long, thin brushstrokes on the back. Using a size 000 brush, paint short lines that follow the curve of the head and apply fine strokes on the breast, underbelly and legs. Finally, sketch in a pencil branch for your bird to perch on.

EURASIAN HOOPOE

Upupa epops

With its feather crown and a zebra-like pattern on the wings, the Eurasian hoopoe is easily recognized for its outlandish appearance.

When drawing the basic form, bear in mind that you are observing the bird from behind and think carefully about perspective.

1

BASIC FORM

Using light pencil strokes, and following the proportions and positions in my sketch, draw a series of shapes that capture the hoopoe's mid-flight form. For reference, my sketch is 15cm wide by 14cm tall (6in x 5½in), with the far wing shape measuring 10cm x 5cm (4in x 2in).

2

REFINED OUTLINE

Sketch a more accurate outline within your shapes. Draw out the feathers on the head. Notice how thin the beak is, and how it curves downwards. Take some time shaping the pointed wing feathers and draw each separate tail feather. Once happy with your outline, erase your basic shapes.

3

PENCIL DETAILS

Using the final image as a reference, draw out different sections of colour. A hoopoe has a wonderfully detailed feather structure with clearly defined colour bands. Make sure you draw them all in. Go over the lines once more, pressing hard to create an indent to use as a border for the paint.

4

PENCIL IMPRESSION

Erase the pencil lines, leaving just the indent and light pencil strokes. Alternatively, if you prefer to leave a few pencil marks on the page, make sure you will be happy with them showing through the paint.

5

HEAD COLOUR

Mix burnt sienna with lots of water and paint a thin layer over the head and plume of feathers. Continue over the upper sections of the outstretched wings.

Brush 1
Burnt Sienna

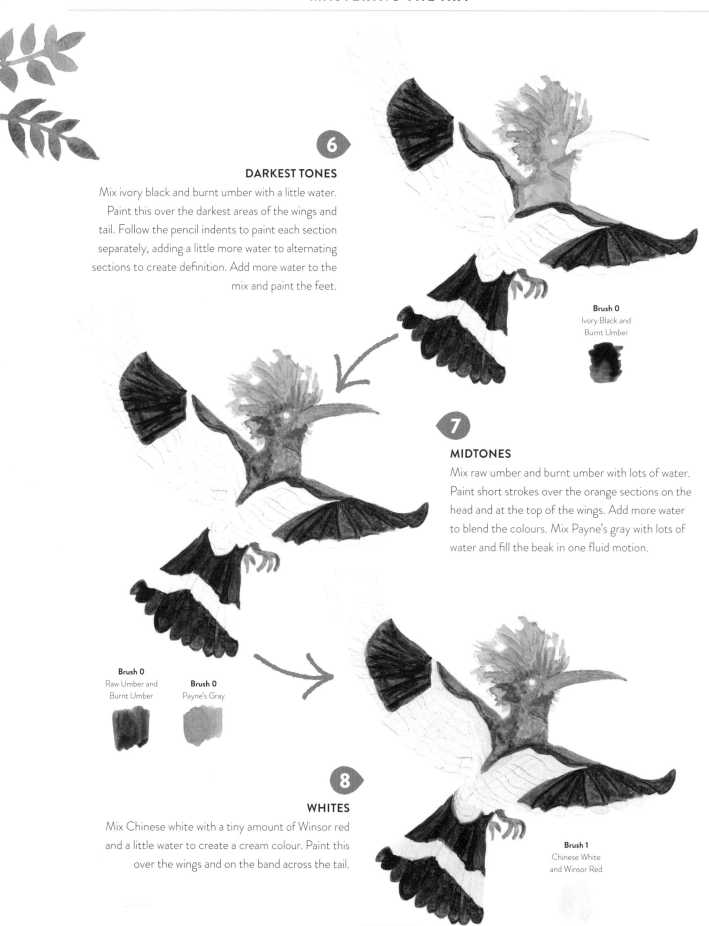

6

DARKEST TONES

Mix ivory black and burnt umber with a little water. Paint this over the darkest areas of the wings and tail. Follow the pencil indents to paint each section separately, adding a little more water to alternating sections to create definition. Add more water to the mix and paint the feet.

Brush 0
Ivory Black and
Burnt Umber

7

MIDTONES

Mix raw umber and burnt umber with lots of water. Paint short strokes over the orange sections on the head and at the top of the wings. Add more water to blend the colours. Mix Payne's gray with lots of water and fill the beak in one fluid motion.

Brush 0
Raw Umber and
Burnt Umber

Brush 0
Payne's Gray

8

WHITES

Mix Chinese white with a tiny amount of Winsor red and a little water to create a cream colour. Paint this over the wings and on the band across the tail.

Brush 1
Chinese White
and Winsor Red

Brush 000
Ivory Black

9

FEATHER DETAILS

Mix a concentrated ivory black to complete the feather details. Paint the tips of all head, wing and tail feathers, and trace the indent lines on the wing and tail feathers. On the white wing sections, paint bands to create a chequerboard effect. Fill in the eye, paint a thin line along the middle of the beak and fill in the ends of the toes for claws. Add lots of water to the mix and wash over the tip of the beak.

10

FINISHING TOUCHES

Mix Winsor orange with a little water and paint long, thin strokes over the head feathers. Add short dashes on the head and the top of the wings. Using white drawing ink and a size 000 brush, paint a white highlight in the eye and a few short strokes radiating out from the eye and into the head feathers. Add a thin line along the top half of the beak and use long strokes to highlight the lines between each of the wing and tail feathers.

Brush 000
Winsor Orange

BLUE JAY

Cyanocitta cristata

The blue jay is famous for its beautiful, brightly coloured plumage. Here, you will use a fine paintbrush to paint the bird's intricate tiger-like markings.

1

BASIC FORM

Using light pencil strokes, and following the proportions and positions in my sketch, draw a series of shapes that capture the jay's mid-flight form. For reference, my sketch is 20cm wide by 13cm tall (8in x 5in). The body measures 3cm x 4cm (1¼in x 1⅗in) and each wing shape is roughly 10cm x 4cm (4in x 1⅗in).

When drawing the basic form, bear in mind that you are observing the bird from above, as if the bird is spread out right below you.

2

REFINED OUTLINE

Sketch a more accurate outline within your basic shapes. Note the tufted feathers on the smallish head and the long, pointed beak. Draw in lots of lines to indicate the many layers of feathers. Once you have an outline you like, erase your basic shapes.

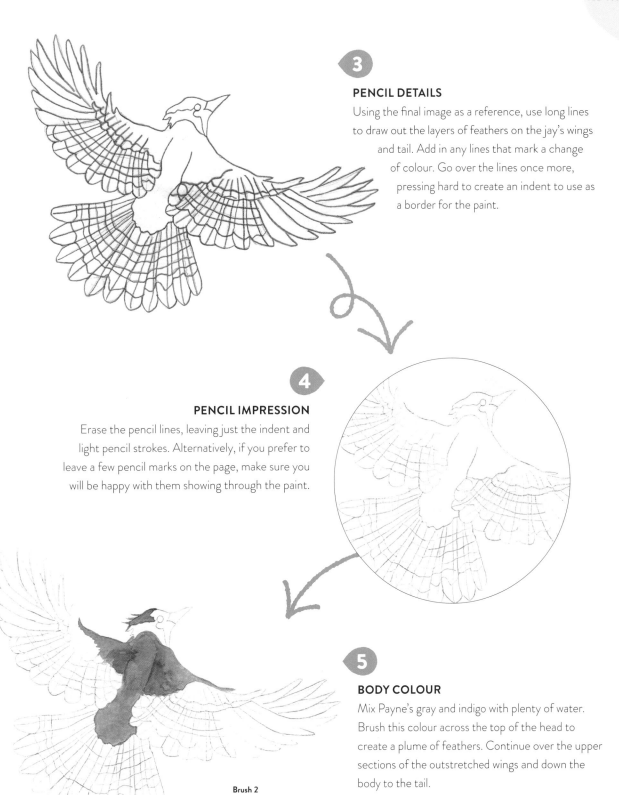

3

PENCIL DETAILS

Using the final image as a reference, use long lines to draw out the layers of feathers on the jay's wings and tail. Add in any lines that mark a change of colour. Go over the lines once more, pressing hard to create an indent to use as a border for the paint.

4

PENCIL IMPRESSION

Erase the pencil lines, leaving just the indent and light pencil strokes. Alternatively, if you prefer to leave a few pencil marks on the page, make sure you will be happy with them showing through the paint.

5

BODY COLOUR

Mix Payne's gray and indigo with plenty of water. Brush this colour across the top of the head to create a plume of feathers. Continue over the upper sections of the outstretched wings and down the body to the tail.

Brush 2
Payne's Gray and Indigo

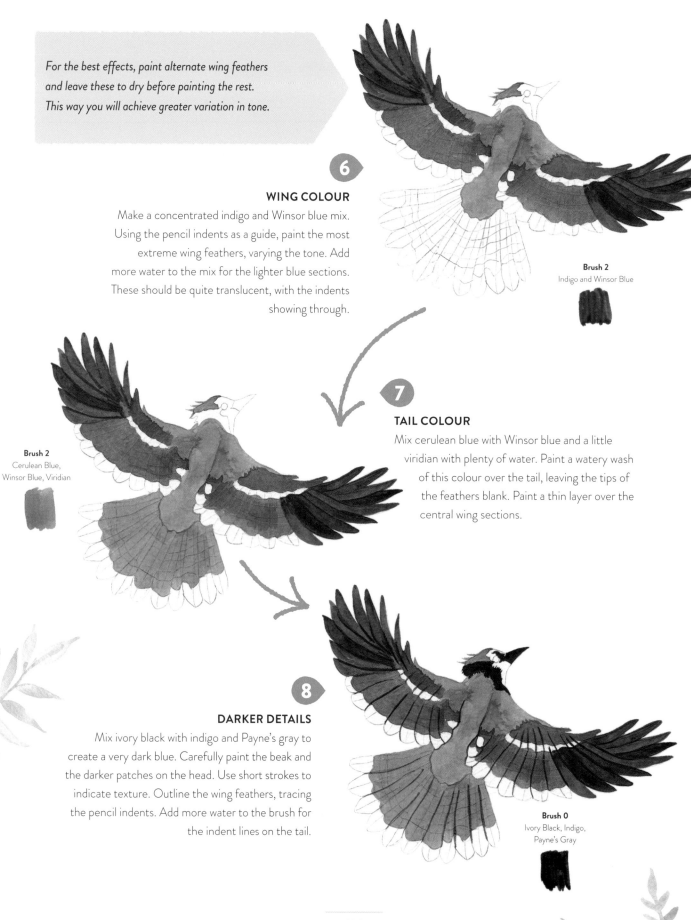

For the best effects, paint alternate wing feathers and leave these to dry before painting the rest. This way you will achieve greater variation in tone.

6

WING COLOUR

Make a concentrated indigo and Winsor blue mix. Using the pencil indents as a guide, paint the most extreme wing feathers, varying the tone. Add more water to the mix for the lighter blue sections. These should be quite translucent, with the indents showing through.

Brush 2
Indigo and Winsor Blue

Brush 2
Cerulean Blue,
Winsor Blue, Viridian

7

TAIL COLOUR

Mix cerulean blue with Winsor blue and a little viridian with plenty of water. Paint a watery wash of this colour over the tail, leaving the tips of the feathers blank. Paint a thin layer over the central wing sections.

8

DARKER DETAILS

Mix ivory black with indigo and Payne's gray to create a very dark blue. Carefully paint the beak and the darker patches on the head. Use short strokes to indicate texture. Outline the wing feathers, tracing the pencil indents. Add more water to the brush for the indent lines on the tail.

Brush 0
Ivory Black, Indigo,
Payne's Gray

9

IRIDESCENCE

Mix French ultramarine with a little water and paint short strokes over the upper wing section and the back. Wash over this layer with water while the paint is still wet, blending the colours. Working quickly, add a little permanent rose to a clean brush and paint a short, thin section down the back, allowing this to blend with the blue.

Brush 0
French Ultramarine

Brush 0
Permanent Rose

10

FINISHING TOUCHES

Mix a concentrated ivory black and draw a circle for the eye. Trace the pencil indents between the feathers and add narrow bands of black to create the tiger-stripe effect. Blend the black in with a little water. Mix Chinese white with a little water and a tiny drop of indigo. Paint the face and the tips of the wing and tail feathers. Add short streaks on the wing and tail feathers and paint a few fine strokes on the body. Add the highlight in the eye.

Brush 0
Ivory Black

Brush 0
Chinese White and Indigo

HUMMINGBIRD

Cynanthus latirostris

The broad-billed hummingbird has beautiful, iridescent plumage.
This project uses the wet-on-wet method to bring it to life.

1 BASIC FORM

Using light pencil strokes, and following the proportions and positions in my sketch, draw a series of shapes that capture the bird's mid-flight form. For reference, my sketch is 20cm wide by 12cm tall (8in x 4¾in).

2 REFINED OUTLINE

Sketch a more accurate outline within your shapes. Note the bird's fanned tail. The head and body are relatively small and the beak is long and thin. Mark the wing and tail feathers and draw little feet at the top of the tail. Once happy with your outline, erase your basic shapes.

3 PENCIL DETAILS

Using the final image as a reference, draw the wing and tail feathers in greater detail and add in any lines that mark a change of colour. Go over the lines, pressing hard to create an indent to use as a border for the paint.

PENCIL IMPRESSION

Carefully erase the pencil lines, leaving just the indent and very light pencil strokes. Alternatively, if you prefer to leave a few pencil marks on the page, make sure you will be happy with them showing through the paint.

Use plenty of water to blend all the colours, dabbing here and there with a paper towel.

IRIDESCENCE

Paint water over the head, body and the top of the wing, leaving the eye area clear. Paint a watery lemon yellow wash over the whole area. While still wet, paint a viridian and lemon yellow mix over the top of the head, on the belly and into the wing. Allow the colours to blend. Paint a watery Prussian blue over the chin, allowing it to blend down into the belly area.

Brush 2
Lemon Yellow

Brush 2
Viridian and
Lemon Yellow

Brush 2
Viridian

Brush 2
Prussian Blue

NEUTRALS

Mix Payne's gray with lots of water. Paint the patch around the eye, blending it in. Add some viridian to the mix and paint over the top of the wing and head. Add a little ivory black to the mix and paint the lower body section, blending it into the yellow. Add more ivory black, and even more water, to paint alternate feathers on the rear wing. Once dry, add slightly more Payne's gray to paint the rest. Add some Winsor violet to the mix and paint the darkest feathers on the near wing. Once dry, add lots of water to the Winsor violet mix and fill in the rest of the near wing.

Brush 2
Payne's Gray

Brush 2
Viridian and
Payne's Gray

Brush 2
Viridian, Payne's Gray,
Ivory Black

Brush 2
Viridian, Payne's Gray, Ivory
Black, Winsor Violet

7

WING AND TAIL FEATHERS

Add a little more ivory black to the Winsor violet mix and trace the indent lines on the underside of the near wing. Paint the centre of the tail section with a wash of water and the tiniest amount of the Winsor violet mix. Paint a transluscent layer of Prussian blue over the tail. Add some indigo to the mix and paint the right half of each tail feather. Paint some of this mix at the top of each left half, allowing it to blend down into the lighter blue, and up into the body on the far left.

Brush 2
Viridian, Payne's
Gray, Ivory Black,
Winsor Violet

Brush 2
Prussian Blue

Brush 2
Prussian Blue
and Indigo

8

FACIAL FEATURES AND FEET

Mix permanent rose with a little water and paint the beak. Add some ivory black to the mix, and while the pink is still wet, paint the tip of the beak, allowing the colours to bleed. Add more pigment to the brush and paint a darker section on top of the beak where it joins the face. Mix a concentrated ivory black to paint the eye. Add more water to the brush and paint two curved feet on the belly. When the beak is dry, use a concentrated permanent rose and ivory black mix to paint a thin line down its length.

Brush 0
Permanent Rose

Brush 0
Permanent Rose
and Ivory Black

Brush 0
Ivory Black

Take care not to lose sight of the bird's iridescence as you add these markings. If the colour starts to look too concentrated, add some more water or dab it with a paper towel.

Brush 0 & 5/0
Prussian Blue, Indigo,
Viridian, Yellow Ochre

9 FINE MARKINGS

Mix Prussian blue, indigo, viridian and yellow ochre with plenty of water to create a deep green. Paint short strokes that start on the head and face and carry on down the body becoming looser and larger. Continue these lines on the iridescent wing section and give the near wing a scalloped edge. Trace the indent lines between the feathers on the far wing. Switch to the 5/0 brush and use the same paint mix and plenty of water to create a series of faint, diagonal lines on the left side of the tail feathers and each of the wing feathers.

10 WHITE HIGHLIGHTS

Using a size 0 brush and white drawing ink, paint a highlight inside the eye and a thin border around it. Draw a line where the beak joins the face. Following the natural curves, add tiny highlights all over the iridescent section. Add a series of crisscrossed lines over the centre of the tail section, brushing into the blue feathers to create texture. Trace the indents on the feathers and add some curved lines on the scalloped edge of the near wing.

KINGFISHER

Alcedo atthis

The common kingfisher is a small and shy bird, but its beautiful,
bright plumage makes it hard to miss when it does appear.

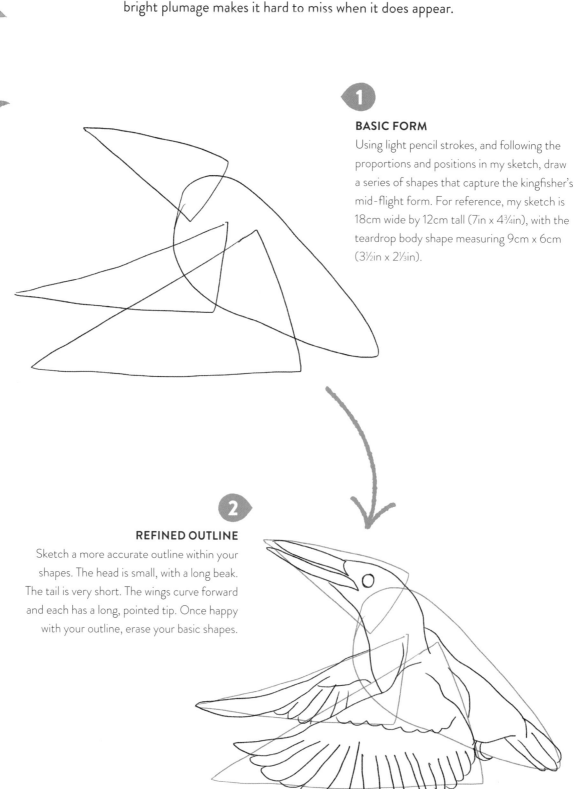

1

BASIC FORM

Using light pencil strokes, and following the
proportions and positions in my sketch, draw
a series of shapes that capture the kingfisher's
mid-flight form. For reference, my sketch is
18cm wide by 12cm tall (7in x 4¾in), with the
teardrop body shape measuring 9cm x 6cm
(3½in x 2⅓in).

2

REFINED OUTLINE

Sketch a more accurate outline within your
shapes. The head is small, with a long beak.
The tail is very short. The wings curve forward
and each has a long, pointed tip. Once happy
with your outline, erase your basic shapes.

PENCIL DETAILS

Using the final image as a reference, draw out different sections of colour, particularly around the head. Add more feather details to the wings and layers on the tail. Go over the lines once more, pressing hard to create an indent to use as a border for the paint.

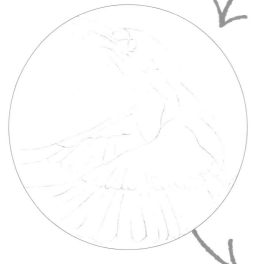

PENCIL IMPRESSION

Erase the pencil lines, leaving just the indent and very light pencil strokes. Alternatively, if you prefer to leave a few pencil marks on the page, make sure you will be happy with them showing through the paint.

BASE COLOUR

Mix viridian, indigo and cerulean blue with plenty of water. Paint a wash over the head, the strip on the chin and the upper wing sections. Vary the amount of water to achieve the different tones. Add a drop more cerulean blue for the tail section.

Brush 2
Viridian, Indigo,
Cerulean Blue

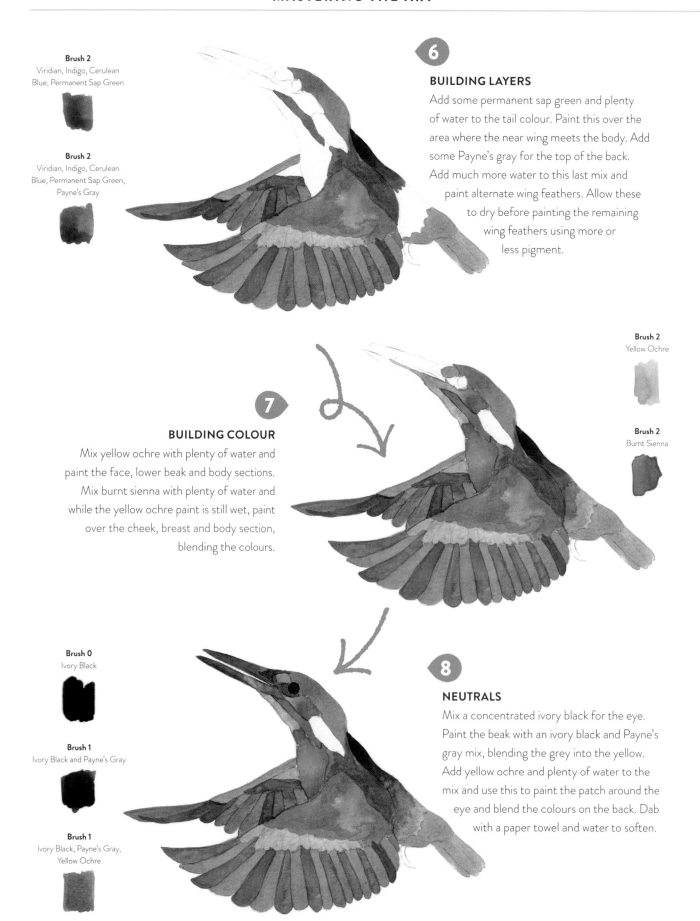

Brush 2
Viridian, Indigo, Cerulean
Blue, Permanent Sap Green

Brush 2
Viridian, Indigo, Cerulean
Blue, Permanent Sap Green,
Payne's Gray

6

BUILDING LAYERS

Add some permanent sap green and plenty
of water to the tail colour. Paint this over the
area where the near wing meets the body. Add
some Payne's gray for the top of the back.
Add much more water to this last mix and
paint alternate wing feathers. Allow these
to dry before painting the remaining
wing feathers using more or
less pigment.

Brush 2
Yellow Ochre

Brush 2
Burnt Sienna

7

BUILDING COLOUR

Mix yellow ochre with plenty of water and
paint the face, lower beak and body sections.
Mix burnt sienna with plenty of water and
while the yellow ochre paint is still wet, paint
over the cheek, breast and body section,
blending the colours.

Brush 0
Ivory Black

Brush 1
Ivory Black and Payne's Gray

Brush 1
Ivory Black, Payne's Gray,
Yellow Ochre

8

NEUTRALS

Mix a concentrated ivory black for the eye.
Paint the beak with an ivory black and Payne's
gray mix, blending the grey into the yellow.
Add yellow ochre and plenty of water to the
mix and use this to paint the patch around the
eye and blend the colours on the back. Dab
with a paper towel and water to soften.

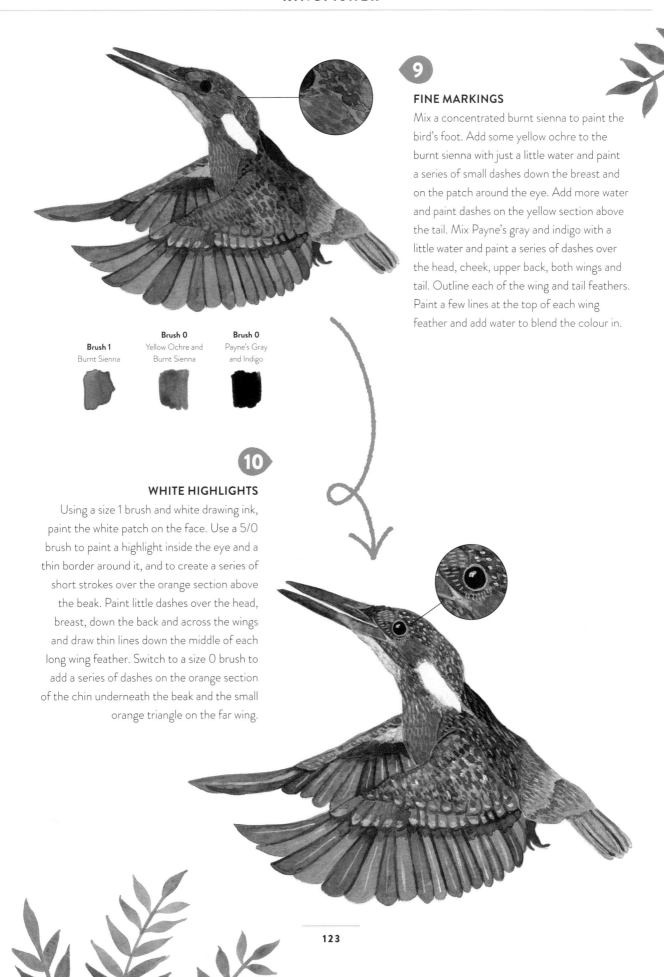

9

FINE MARKINGS

Mix a concentrated burnt sienna to paint the bird's foot. Add some yellow ochre to the burnt sienna with just a little water and paint a series of small dashes down the breast and on the patch around the eye. Add more water and paint dashes on the yellow section above the tail. Mix Payne's gray and indigo with a little water and paint a series of dashes over the head, cheek, upper back, both wings and tail. Outline each of the wing and tail feathers. Paint a few lines at the top of each wing feather and add water to blend the colour in.

Brush 1
Burnt Sienna

Brush 0
Yellow Ochre and
Burnt Sienna

Brush 0
Payne's Gray
and Indigo

10

WHITE HIGHLIGHTS

Using a size 1 brush and white drawing ink, paint the white patch on the face. Use a 5/0 brush to paint a highlight inside the eye and a thin border around it, and to create a series of short strokes over the orange section above the beak. Paint little dashes over the head, breast, down the back and across the wings and draw thin lines down the middle of each long wing feather. Switch to a size 0 brush to add a series of dashes on the orange section of the chin underneath the beak and the small orange triangle on the far wing.

RESOURCES

ART MATERIALS

CASS ART
cassart.co.uk
I purchase the majority of my painting equipment from the art shop Cass Art. The watercolour paper, paint set, drawing inks and paintbrushes used in this book were all purchased from Cass Art. Their blog is also very insightful!

WINSOR & NEWTON
winsornewton.com/uk/education/guides
The paint palette I use is the Winsor & Newton Professional Watercolour set. The Winsor & Newton website is very useful and has a range of great guides.

INSPIRATION

NATURE GUIDES
I love collecting vintage scientific guides on British wildlife. A personal favourite is the Observer's book series, published by Frederick Warne & Co, and available in a huge range of titles. I often find these beautifully illustrated nature guides in vintage shops, charity shops or on eBay.

RSPB
rspb.org.uk/birds-and-wildlife
The RSPB has published numerous books on British Birds over the years. My copy of The Book of British Birds by J. T. R. Sharrock and Peter Holden has proved a valuable source of information and has photographs that are perfect for practicing painting from. The RSPB website is also very useful.

LITTLE PAISLEY DESIGNS
littlepaisleydesigns.com
If you would like to see more of my watercolour bird illustrations, have a look at my website.

FURTHER READING

Birch, Helen, *Just Add Watercolour*, White Lion Publishing, 2019.

Faull, Emma, *Birds: The Watercolour Art Pad*, Mitchell Beazley, 2019.

Forkner, Andrew, *A–Z of Bird Portraits*, Search Press, 2019.

Pond, Tim, *The Field Guide to Drawing and Sketching Animals*, Search Press, 2019.

Putt, Katie, *Boost Your Watercolour Confidence*, Search Press, 2021.

Woodin, Mary, *10 Step Drawing: Nature*, Search Press, 2020.

Zlatkis, Geninne D, *Geninne's Art: Birds in Watercolour, Collage and Ink*, Quarry Books, 2018.

INDEX

ABOUT THE AUTHOR

Eleanor Longhurst is a professional creative living in Bristol. She has run the illustrative nature-inspired brand Little Paisley Designs since 2014, and works from her sunny, plant-filled home studio, assisted by a needy cat and fuelled by lots of cups of tea! This book is a culmination of years spent painting flora and fauna and a wish to share her love of watercolours and birds!

AUTHOR ACKNOWLEDGEMENTS

For my lovely auntie, forever my number one fan, you would have been so proud to see this book.

To my parents and sister for their unwavering support, for encouraging me to start my own business, always helping as unpaid interns, and tolerating a huge amount of stock lying around the house in those early days. Without you, none of this would have been possible!

To my indie business girl gang – the Christmas Ruiners – for always having my back, pepping me up, and for the constant crisp chat.

Thank you.